Mandalas

Adult Stress Relief

Coloring Book

This book belongs to:

Relax and color the stress away.

Color Test Page

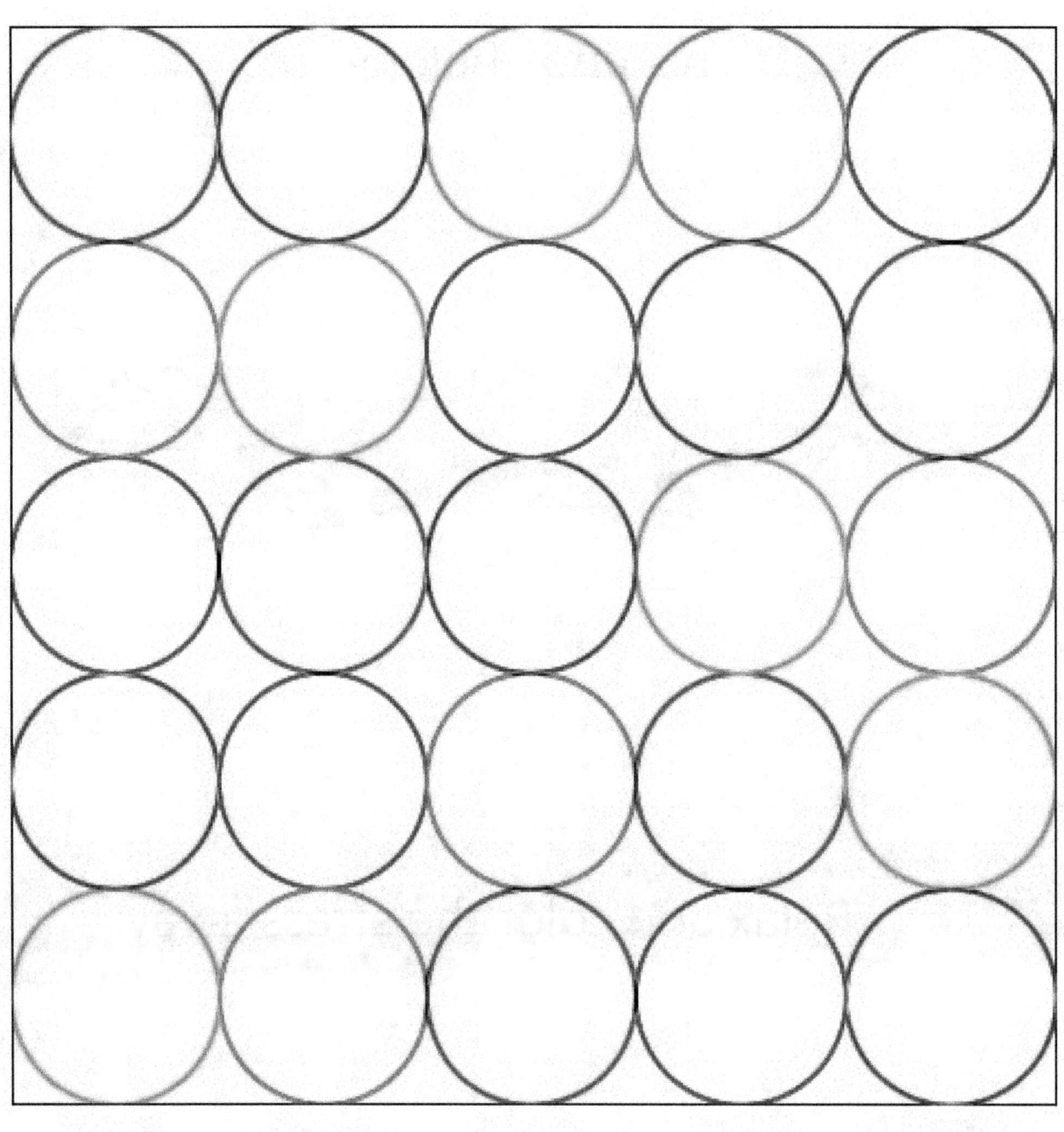

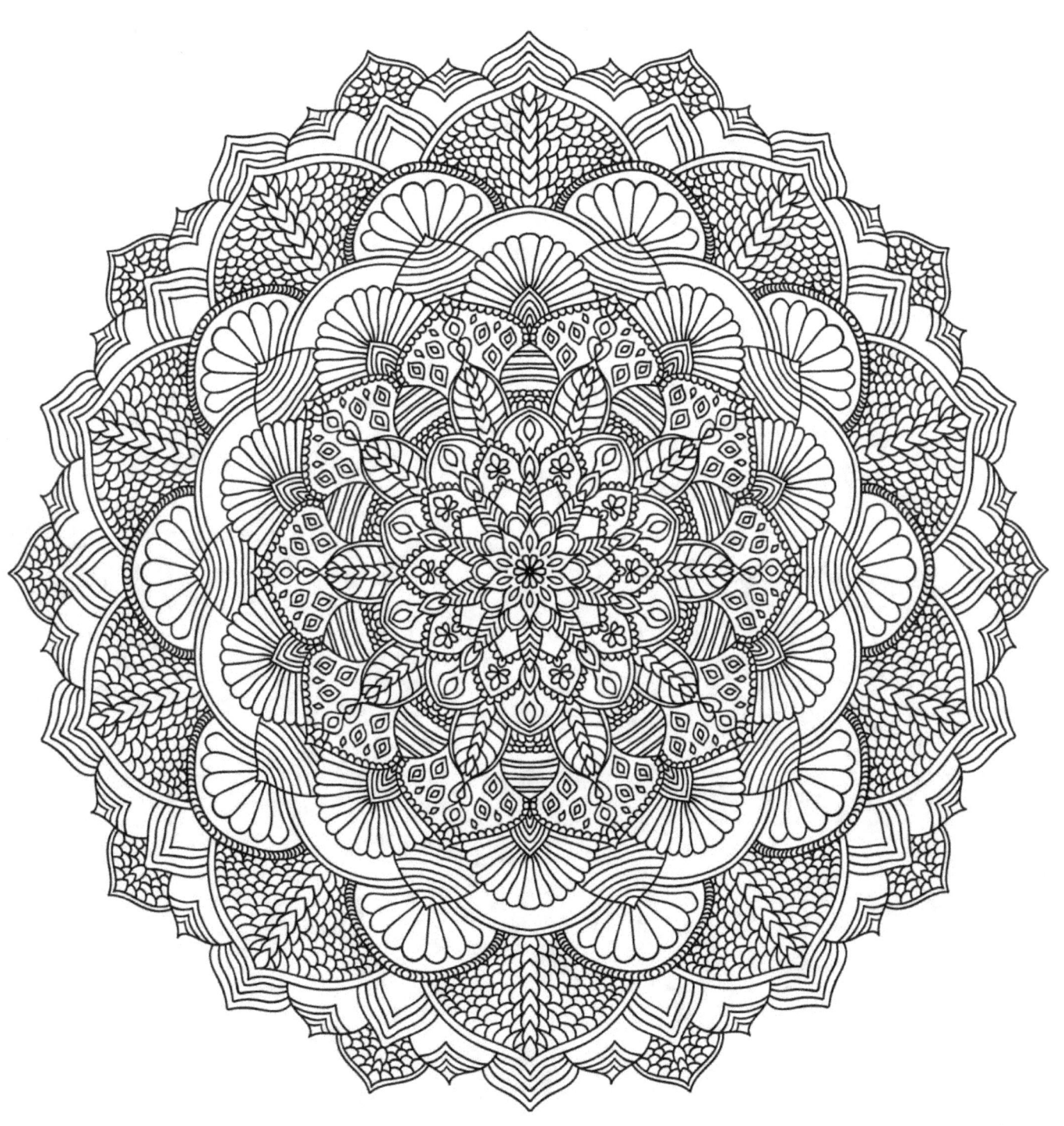

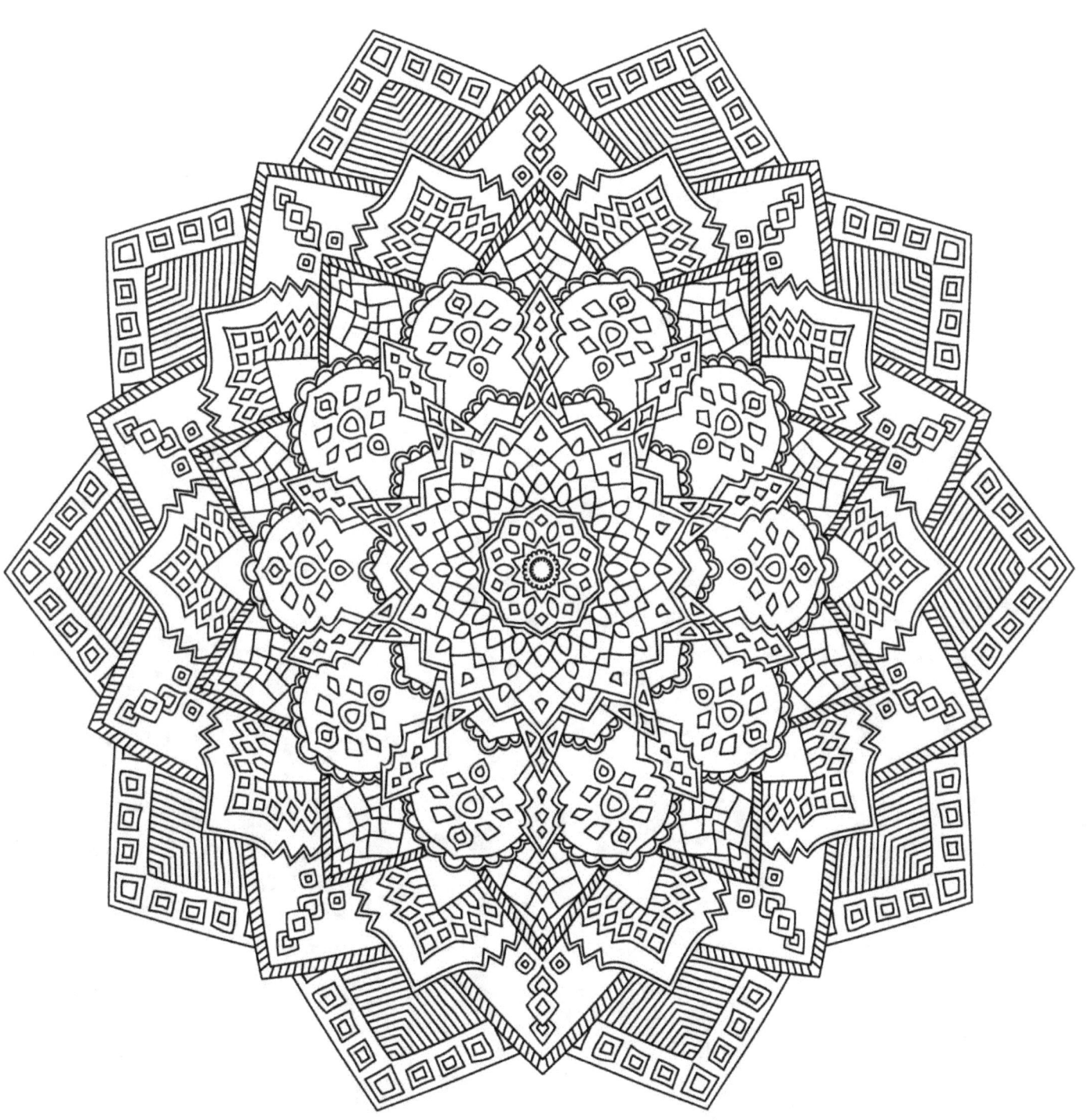

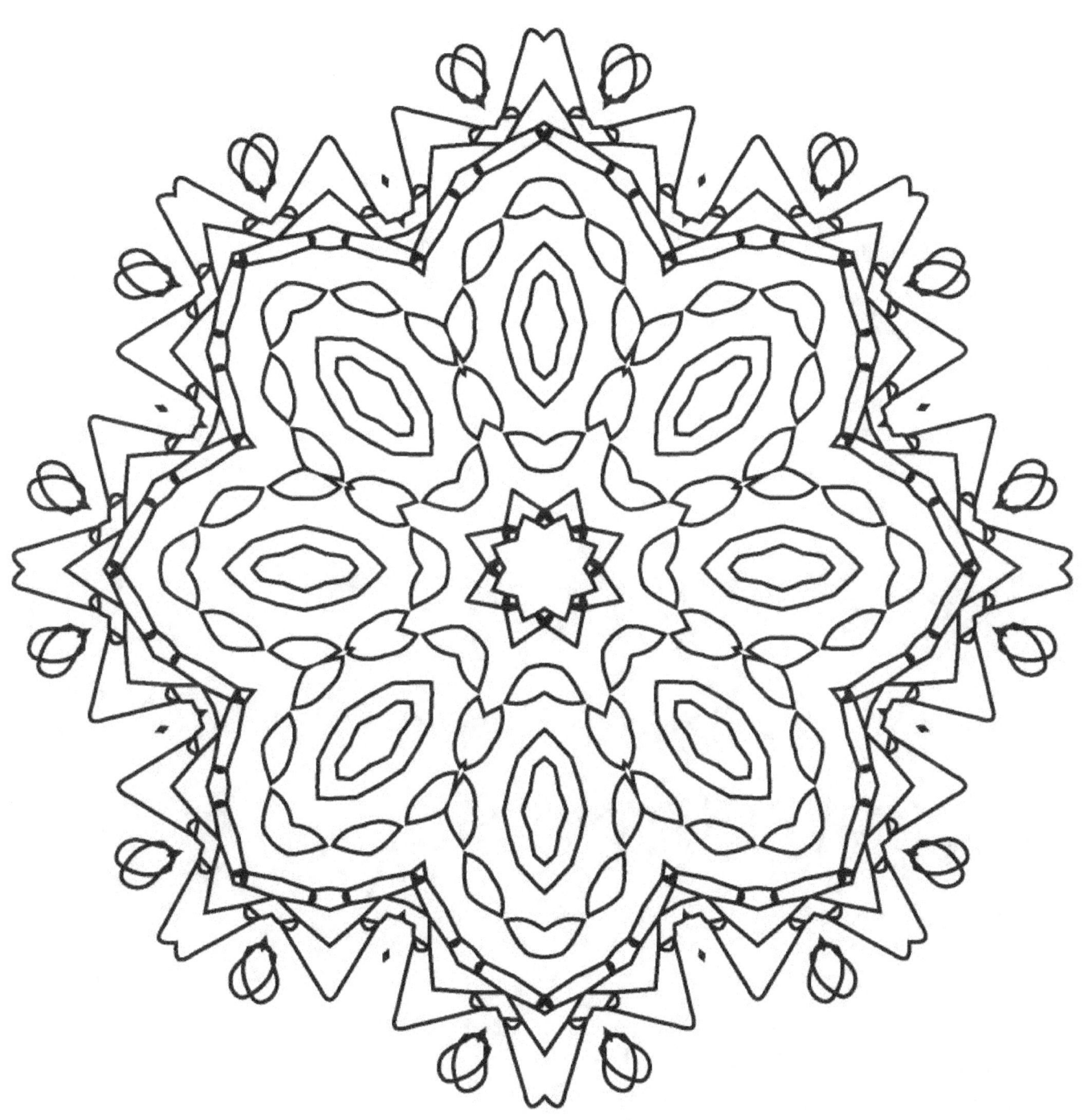

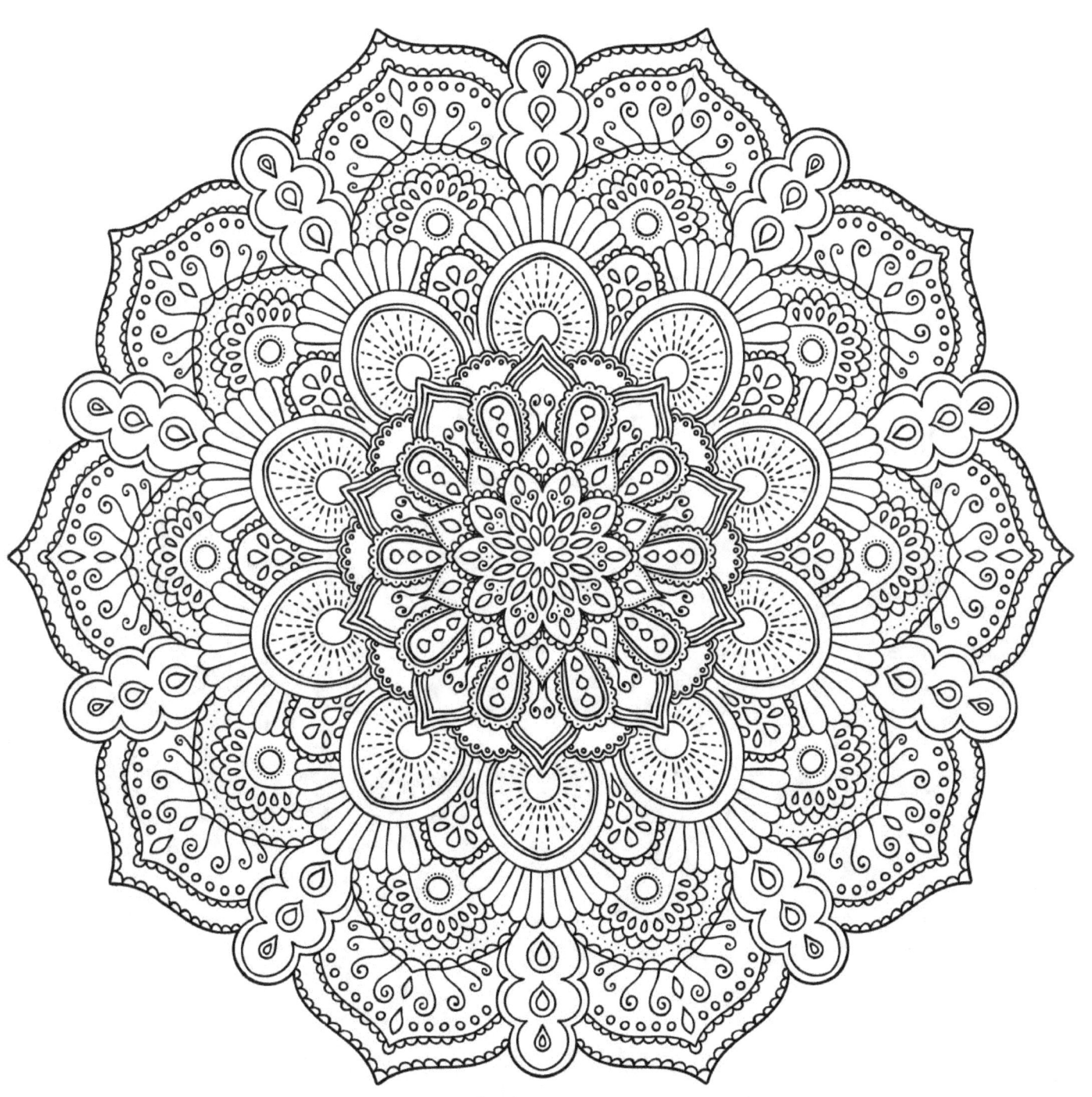

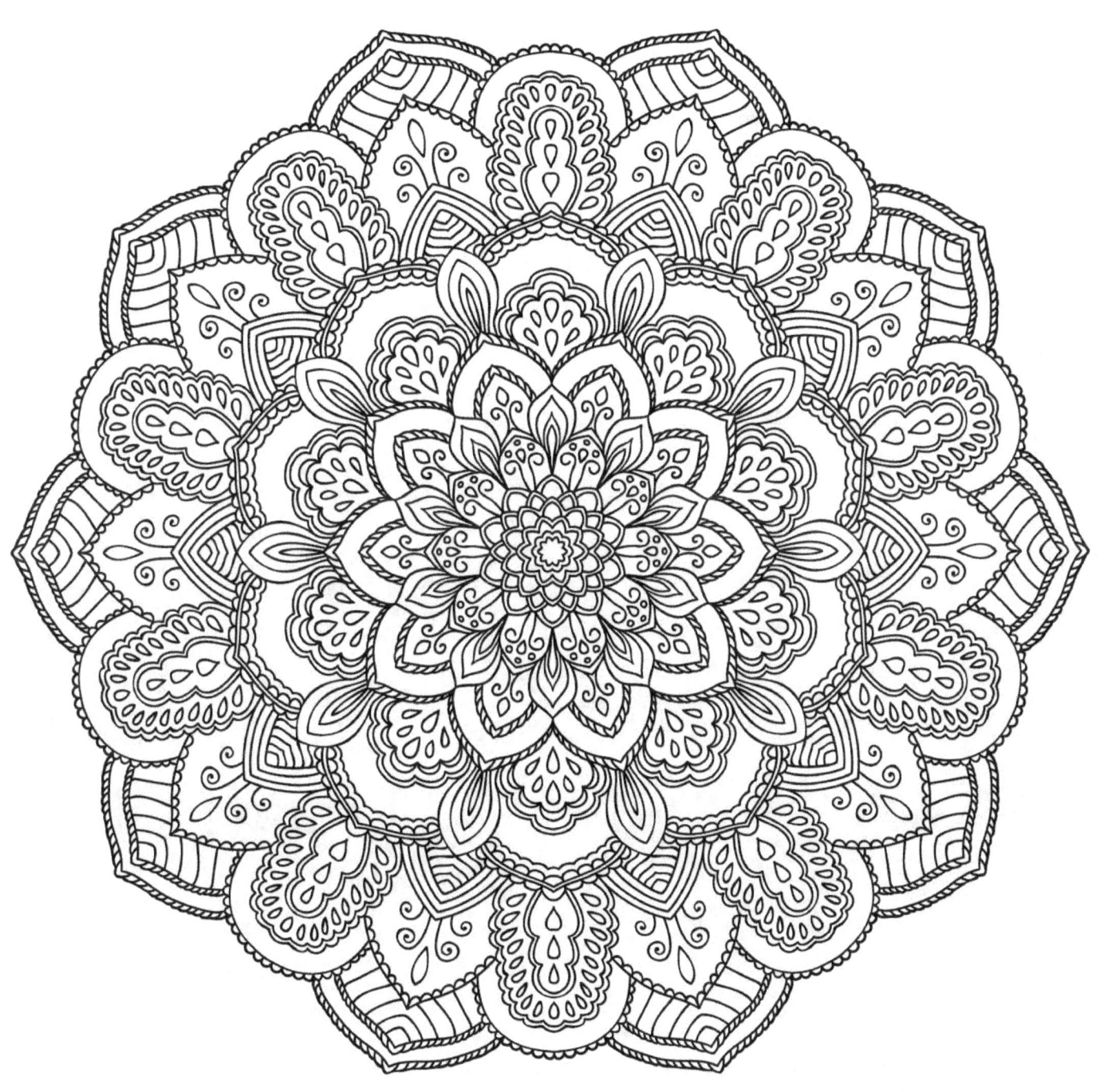

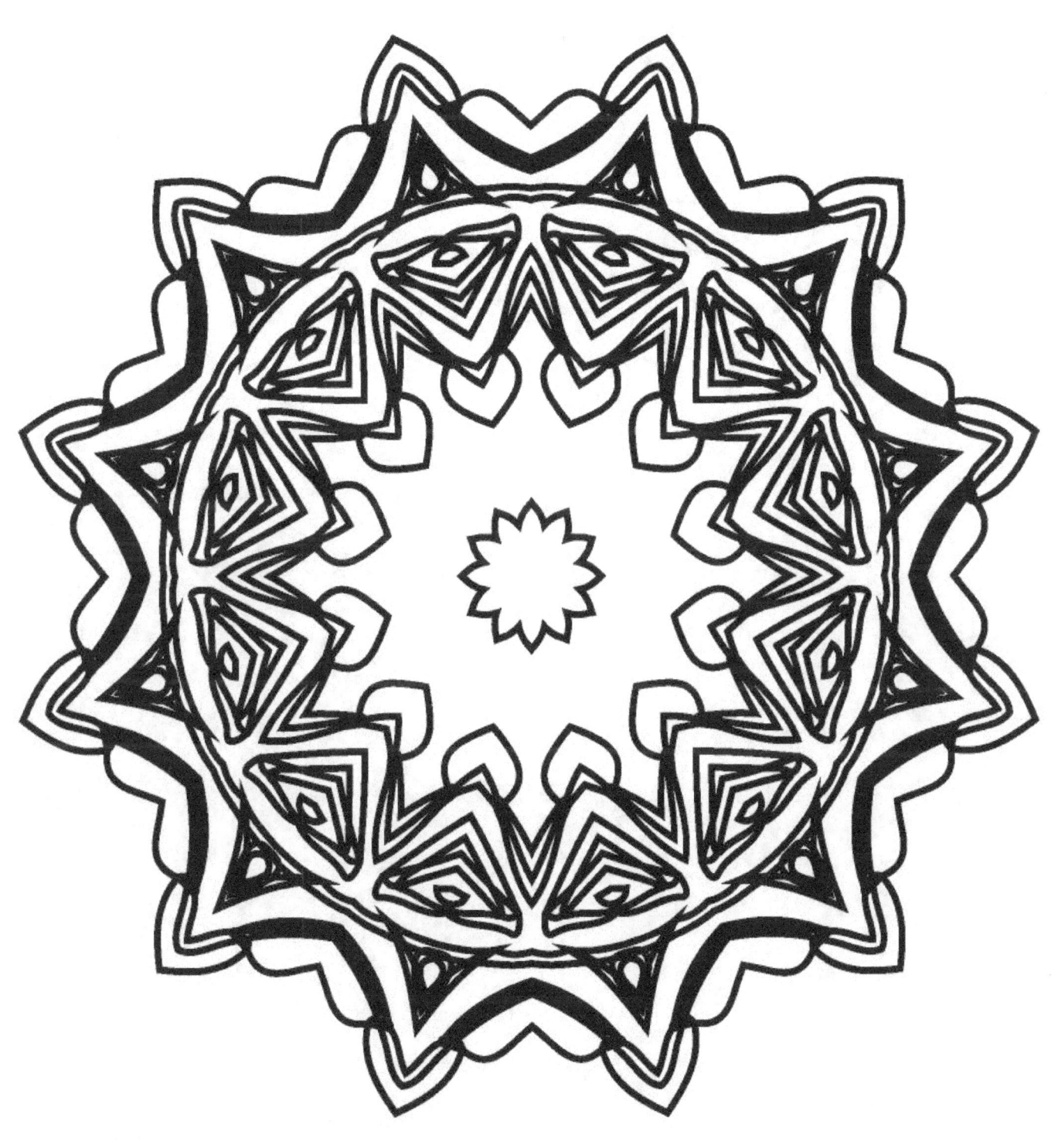

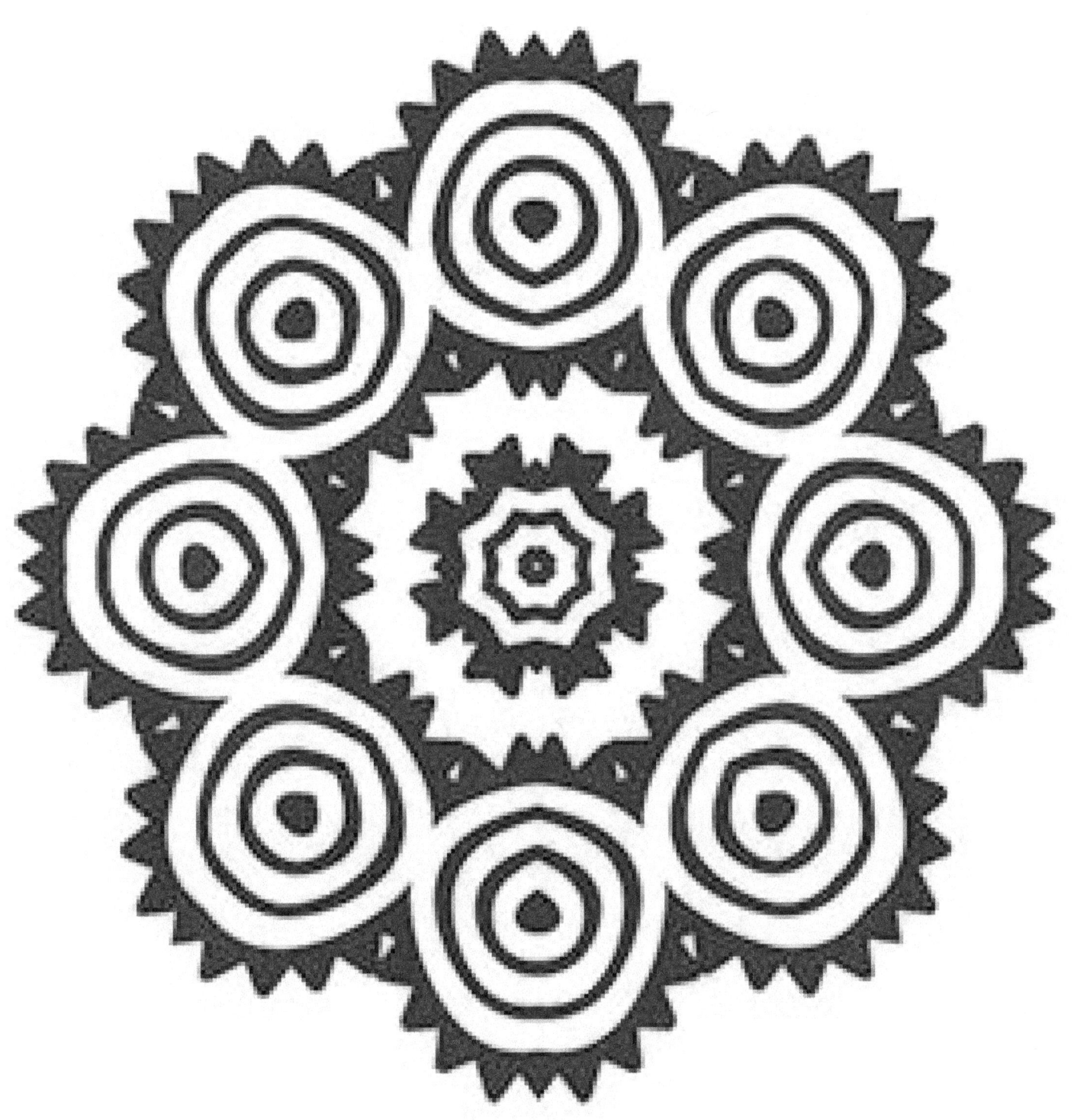

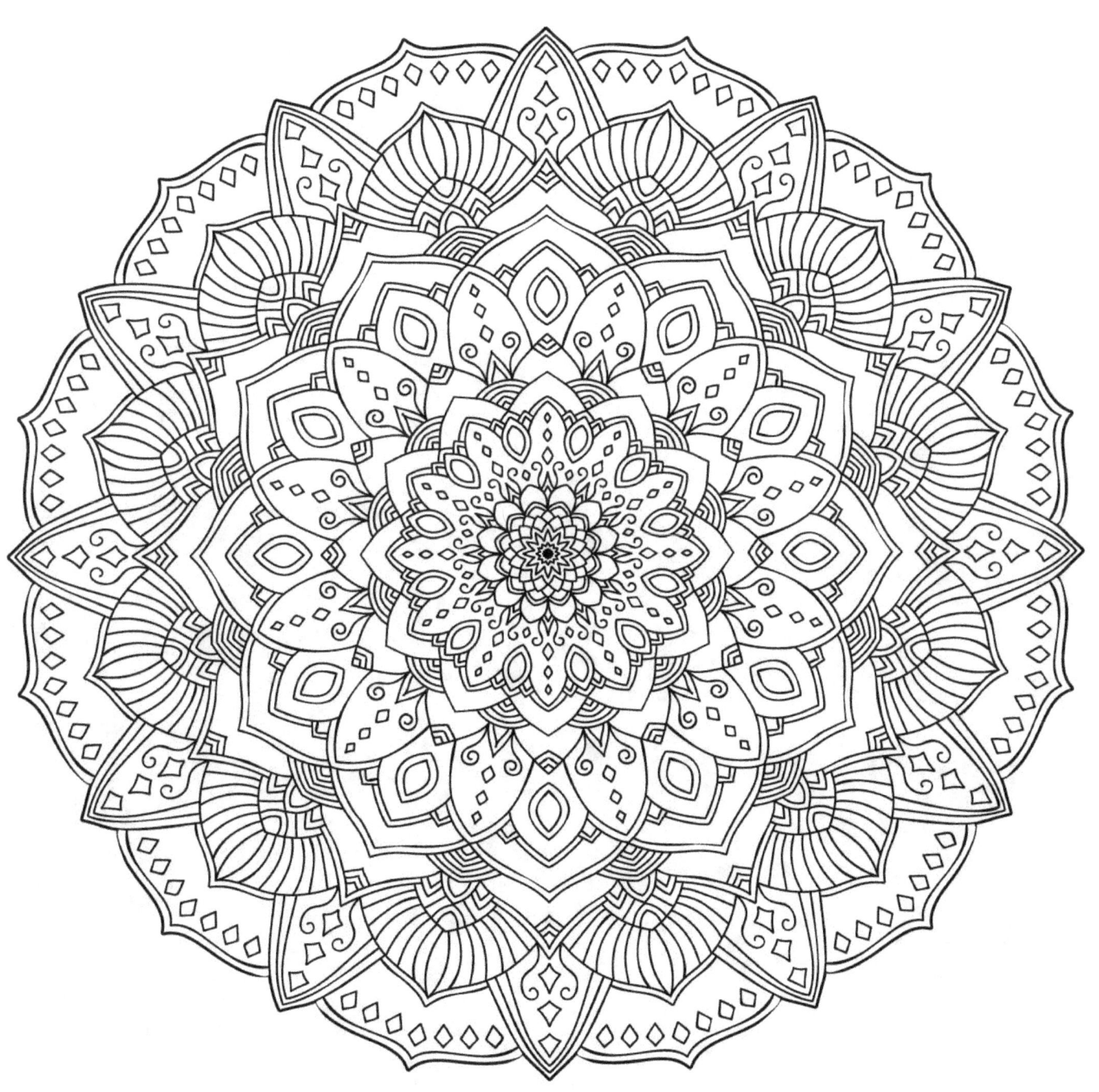

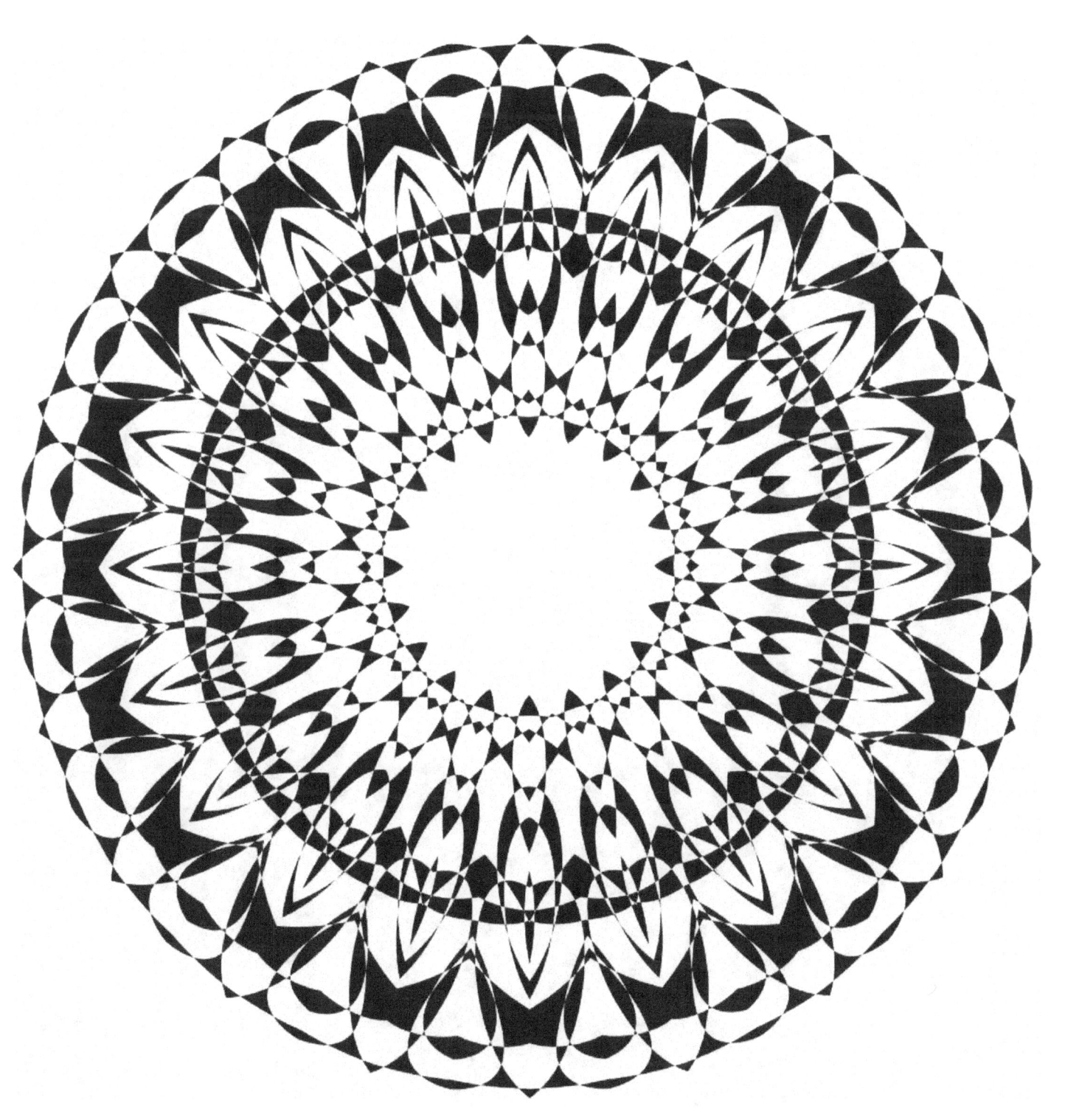

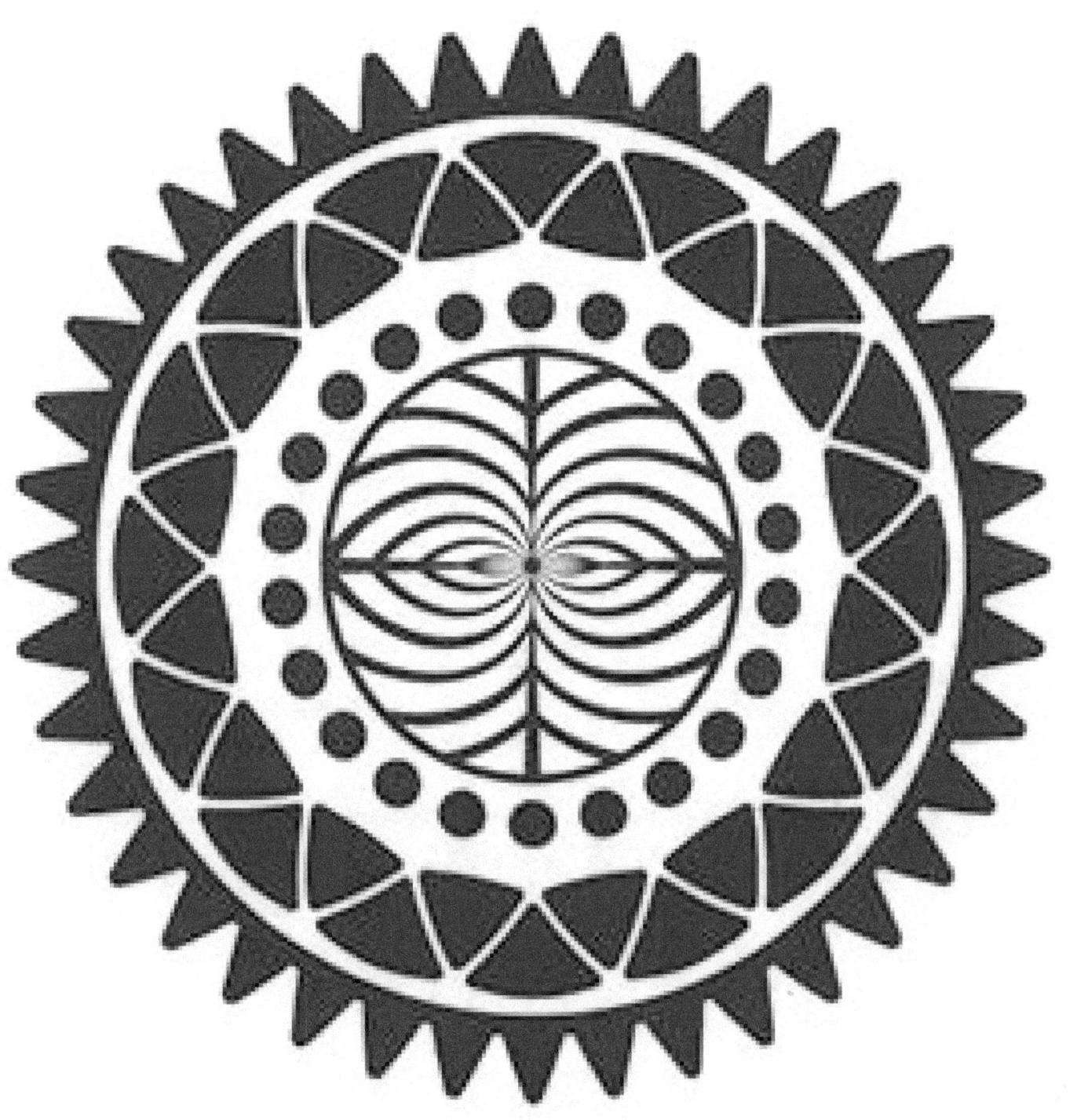

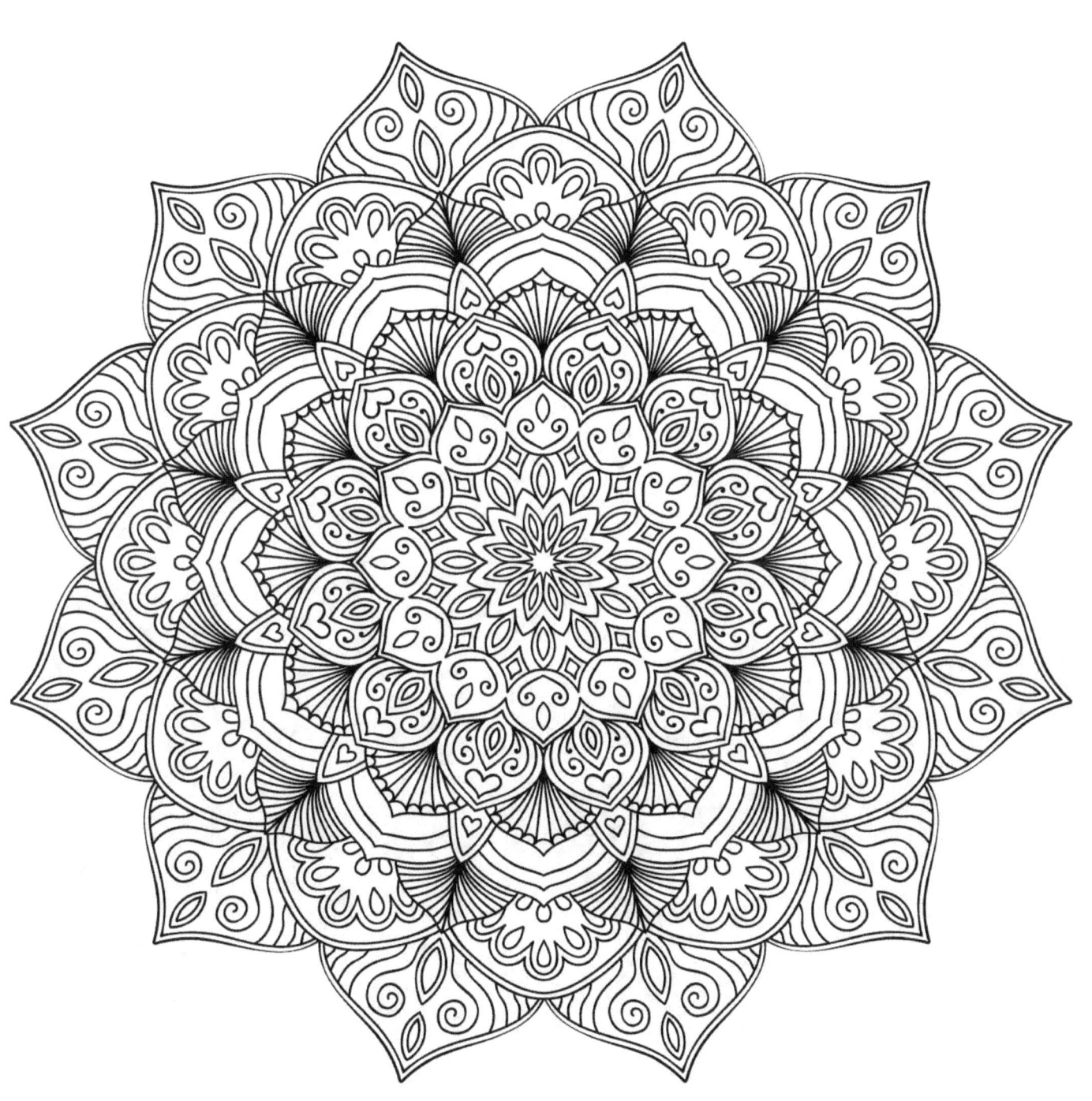

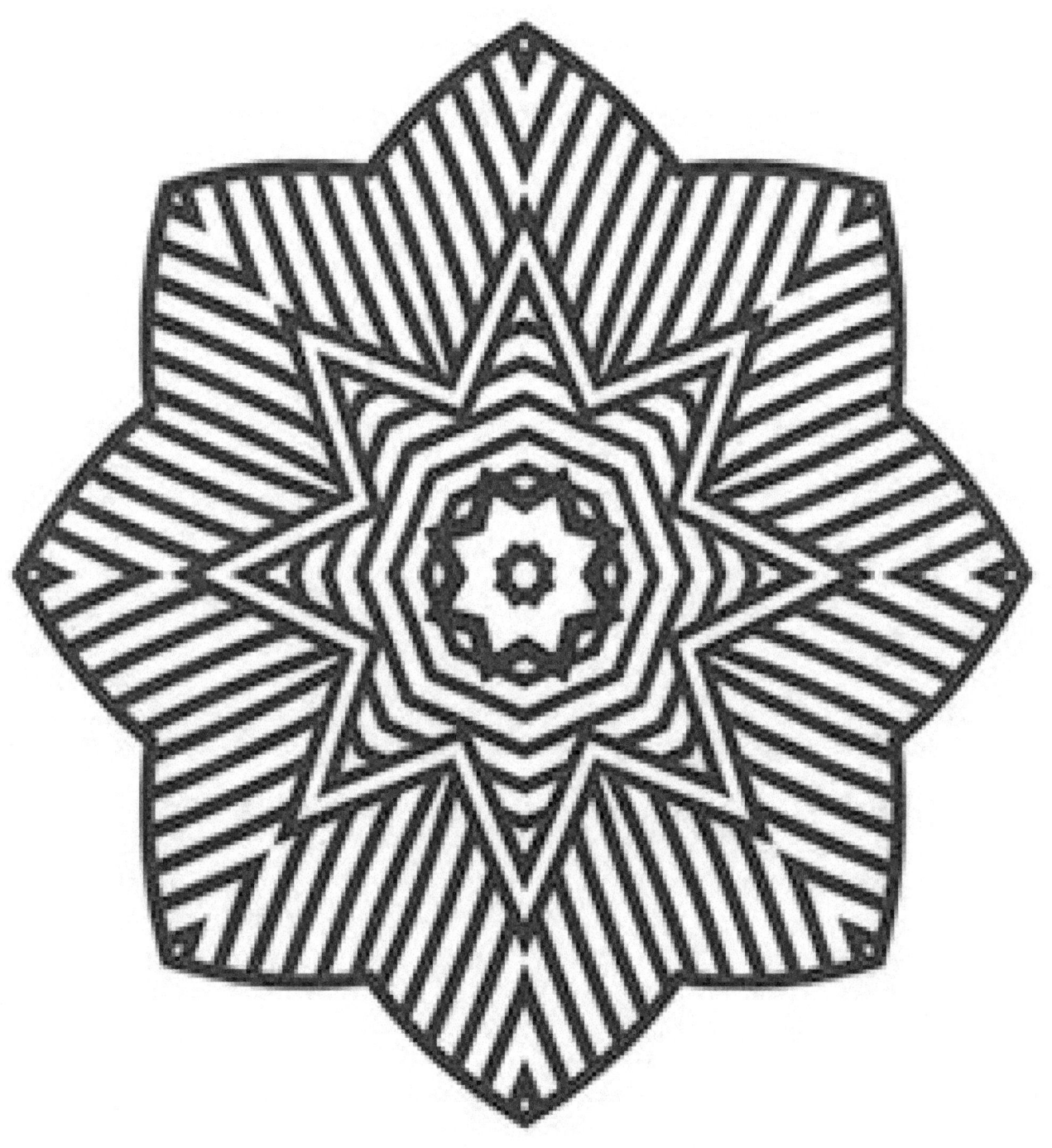

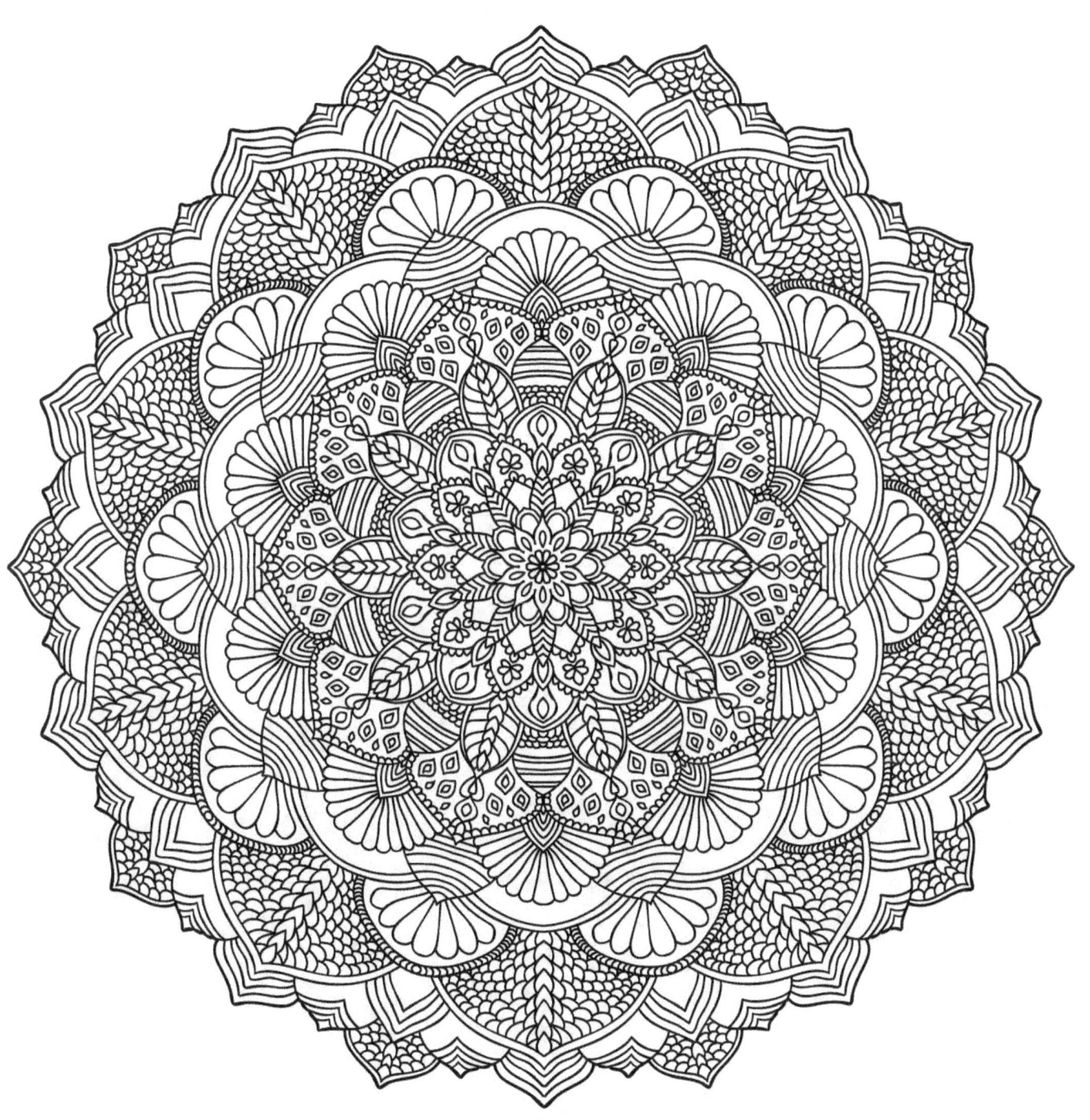

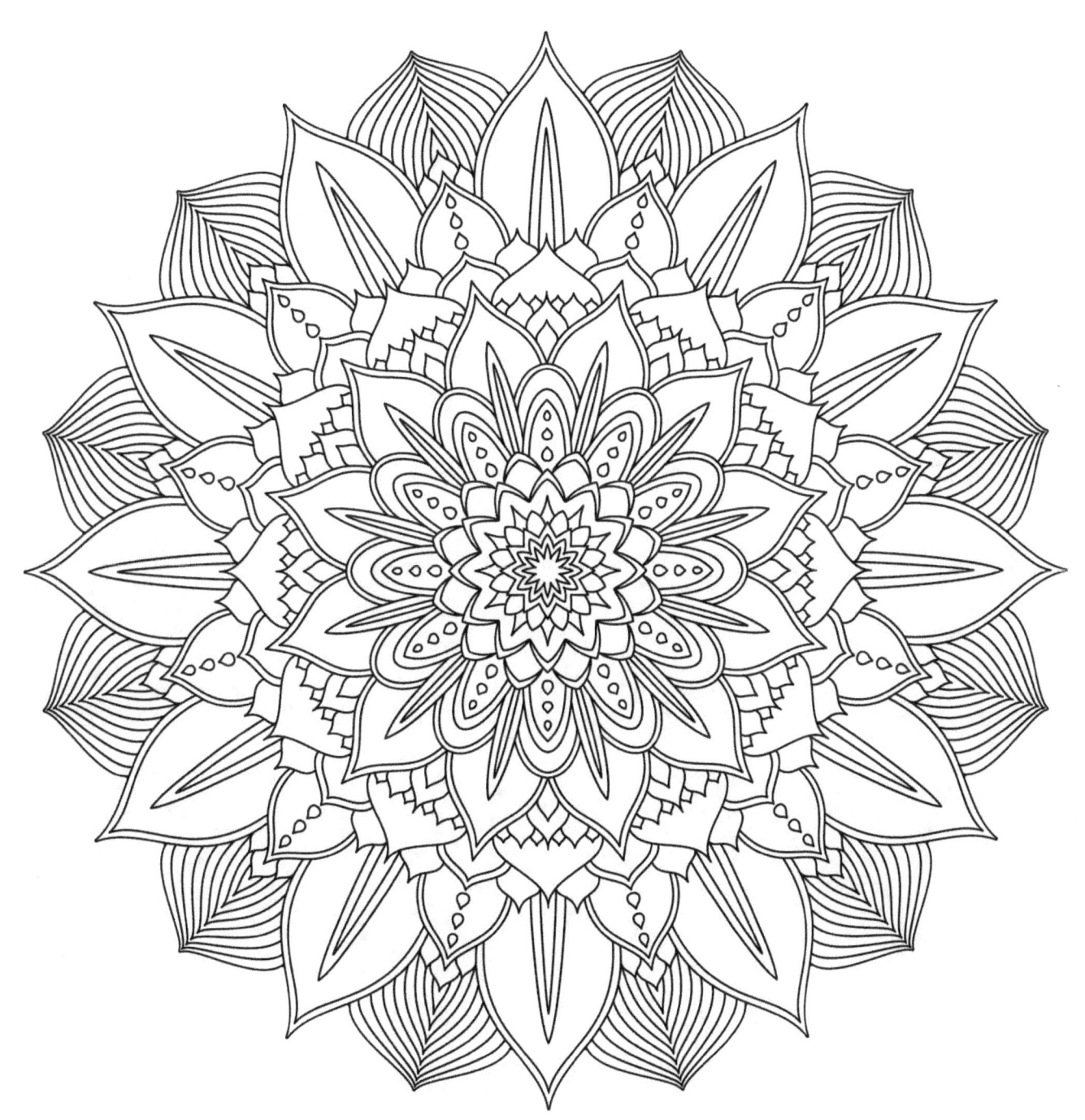

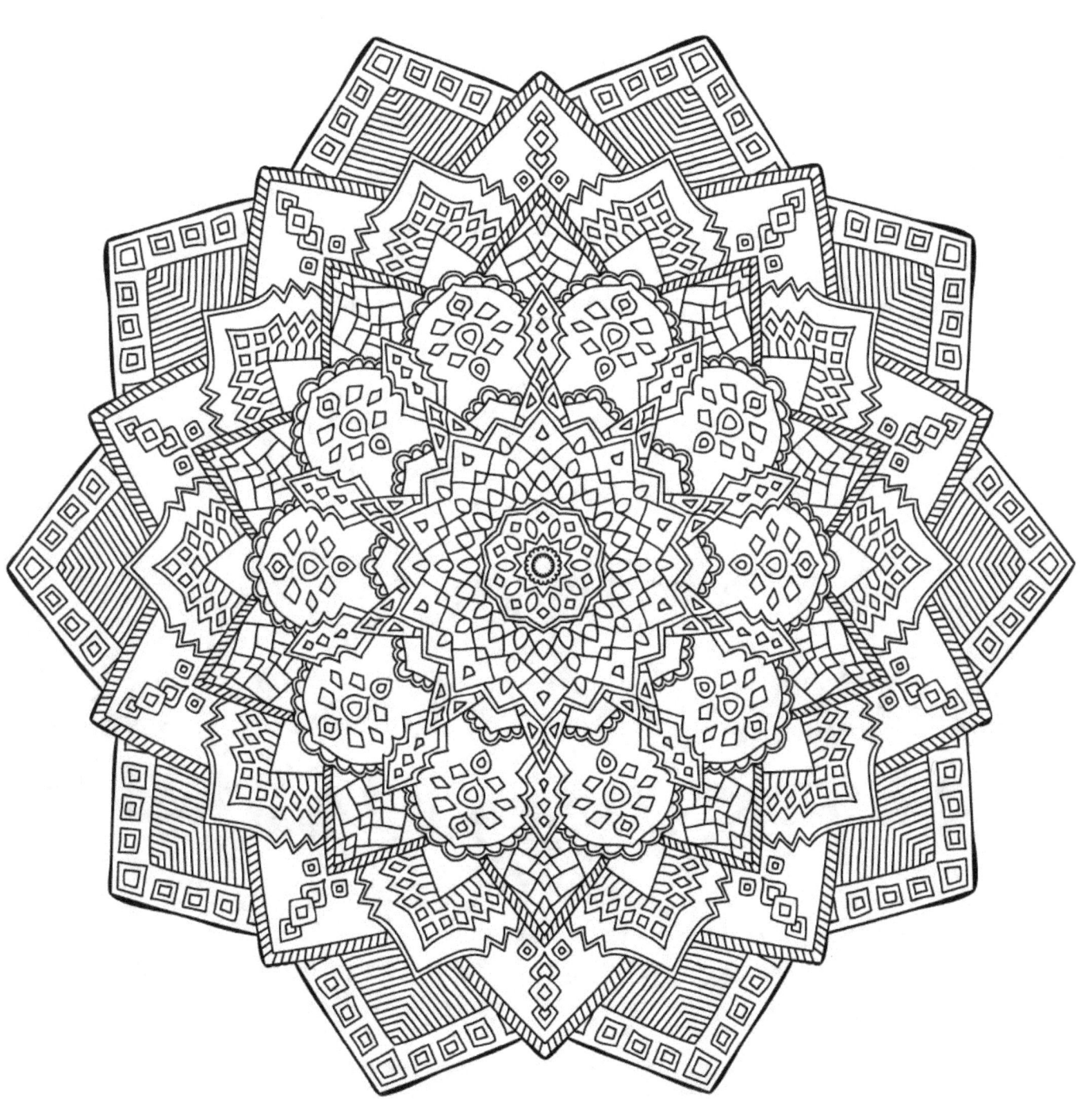

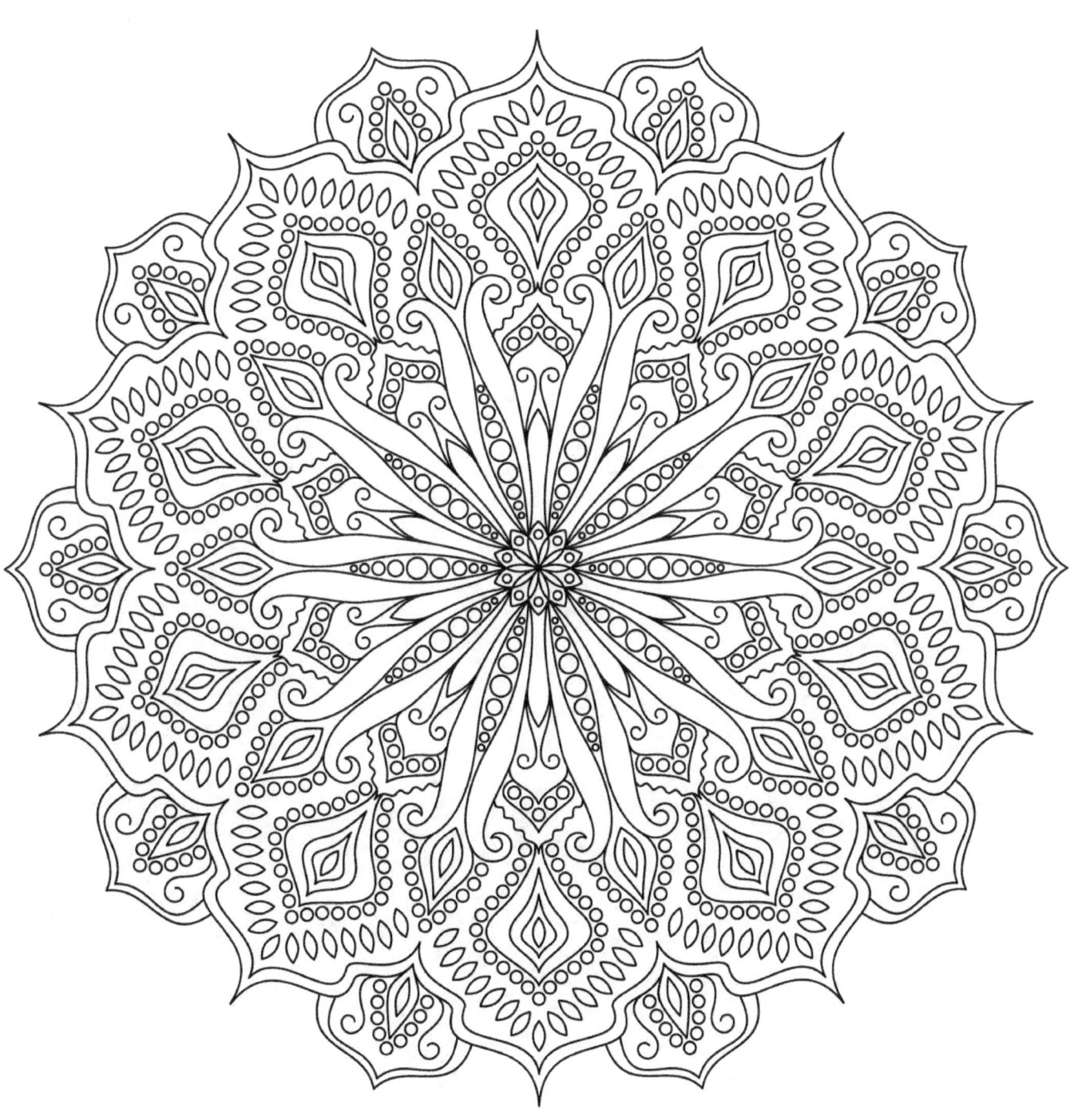

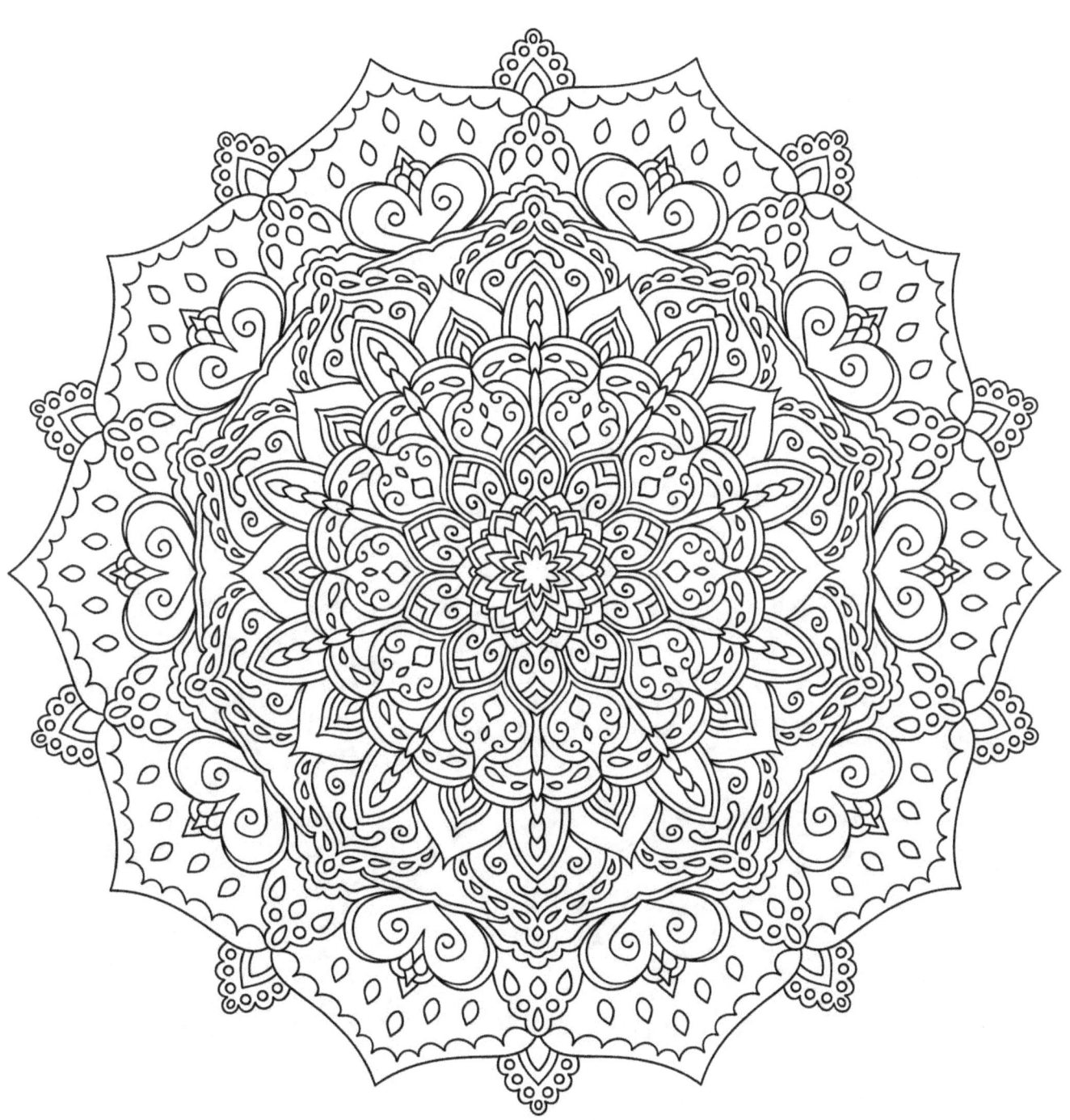

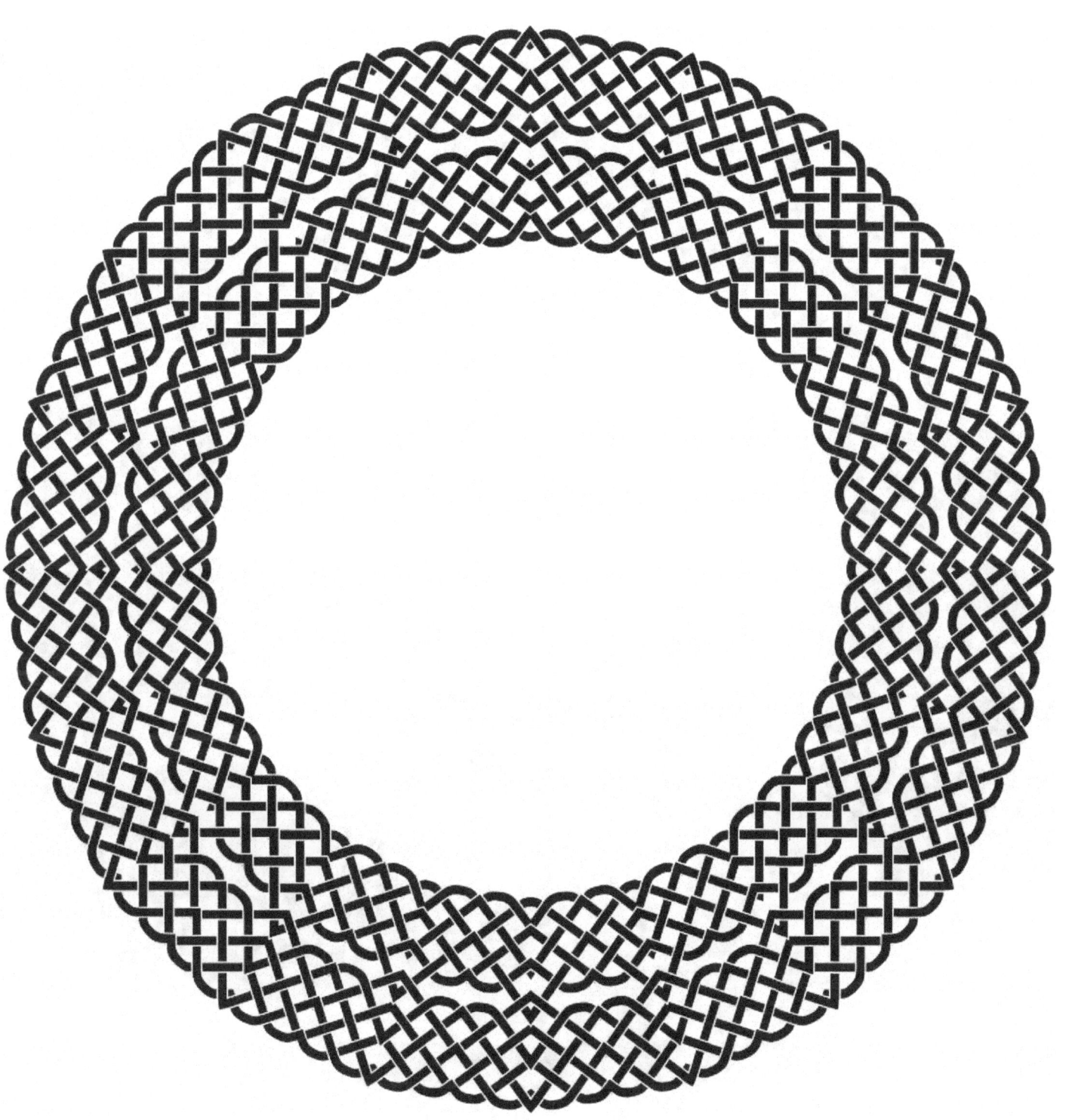

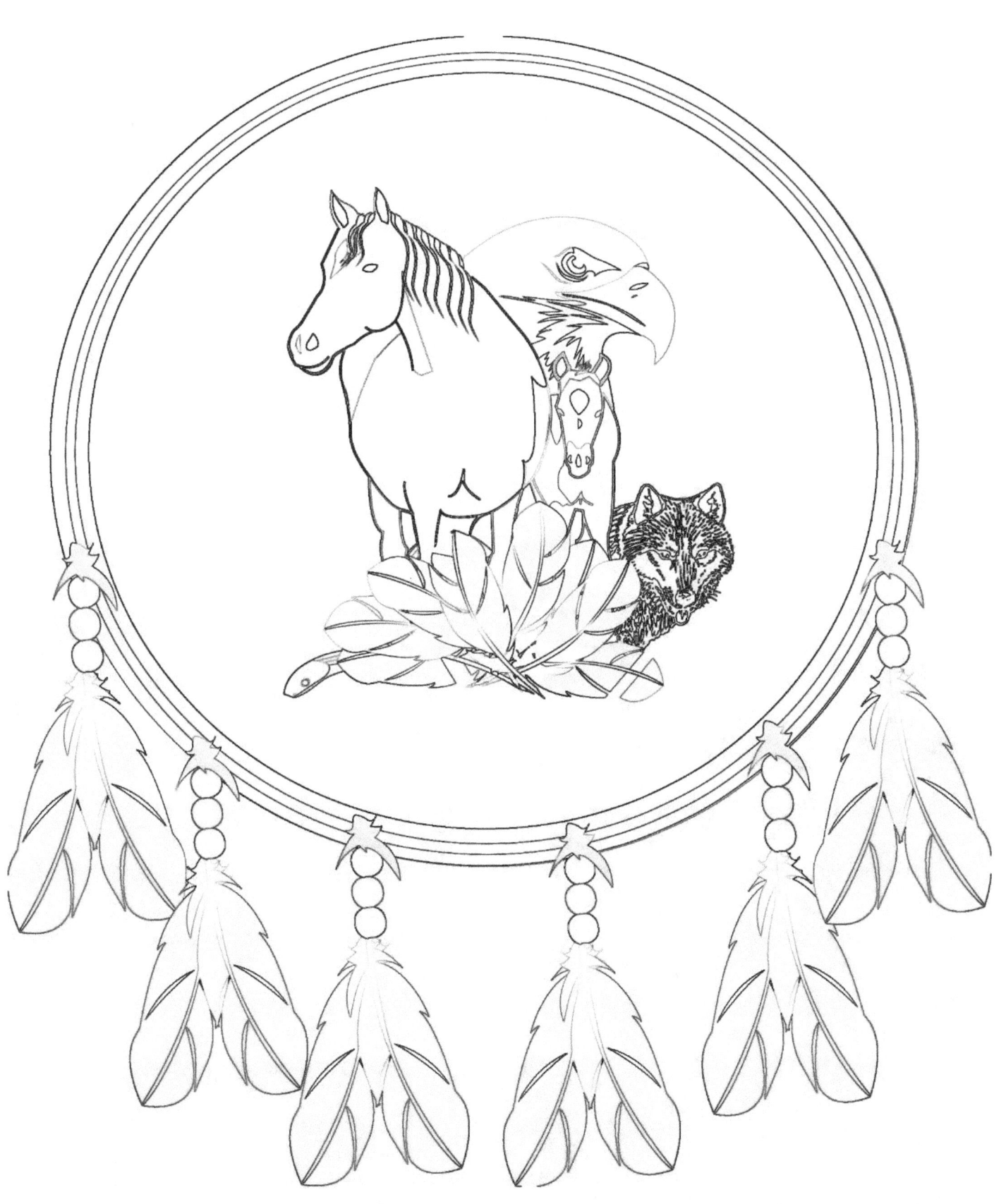

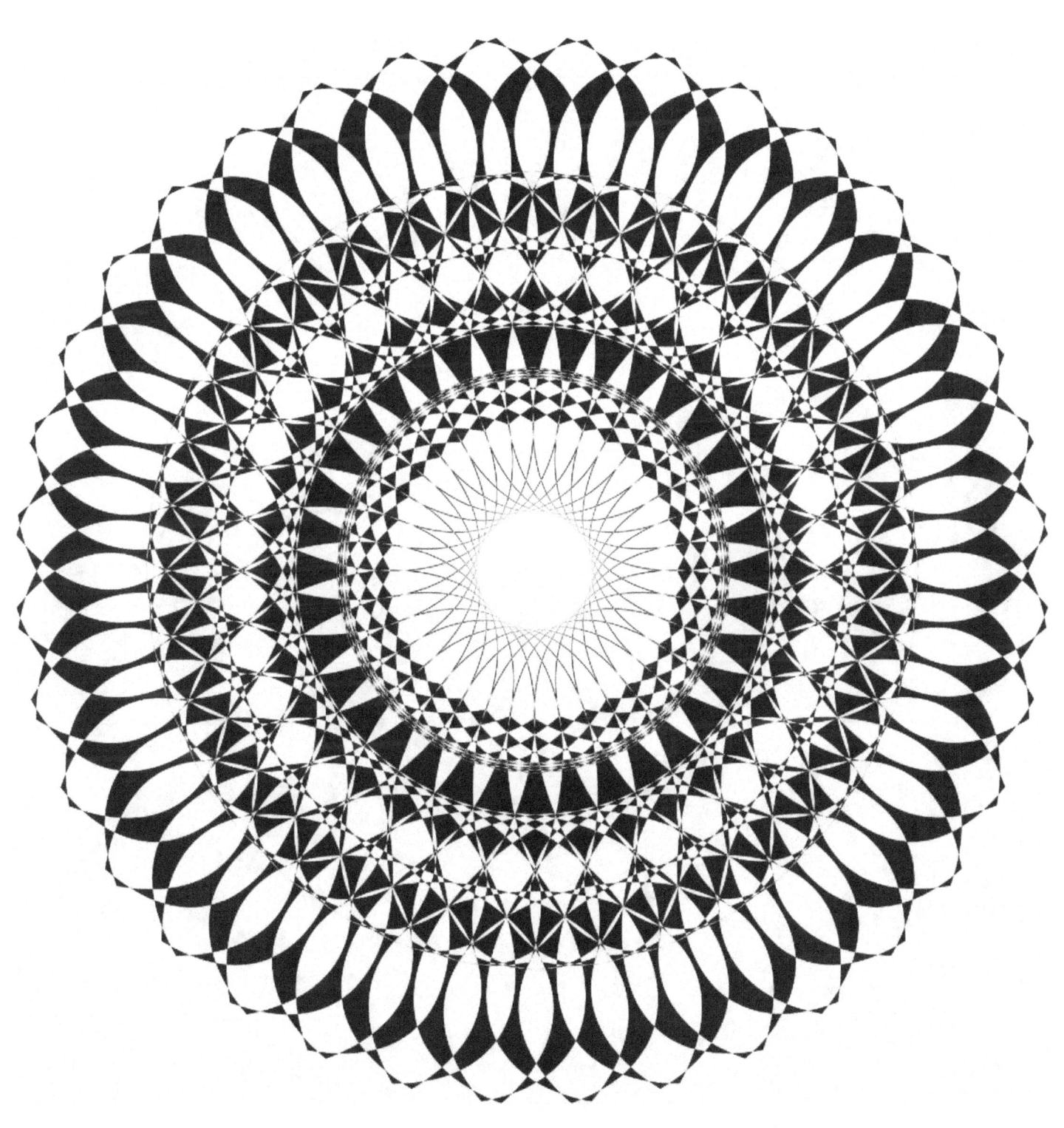

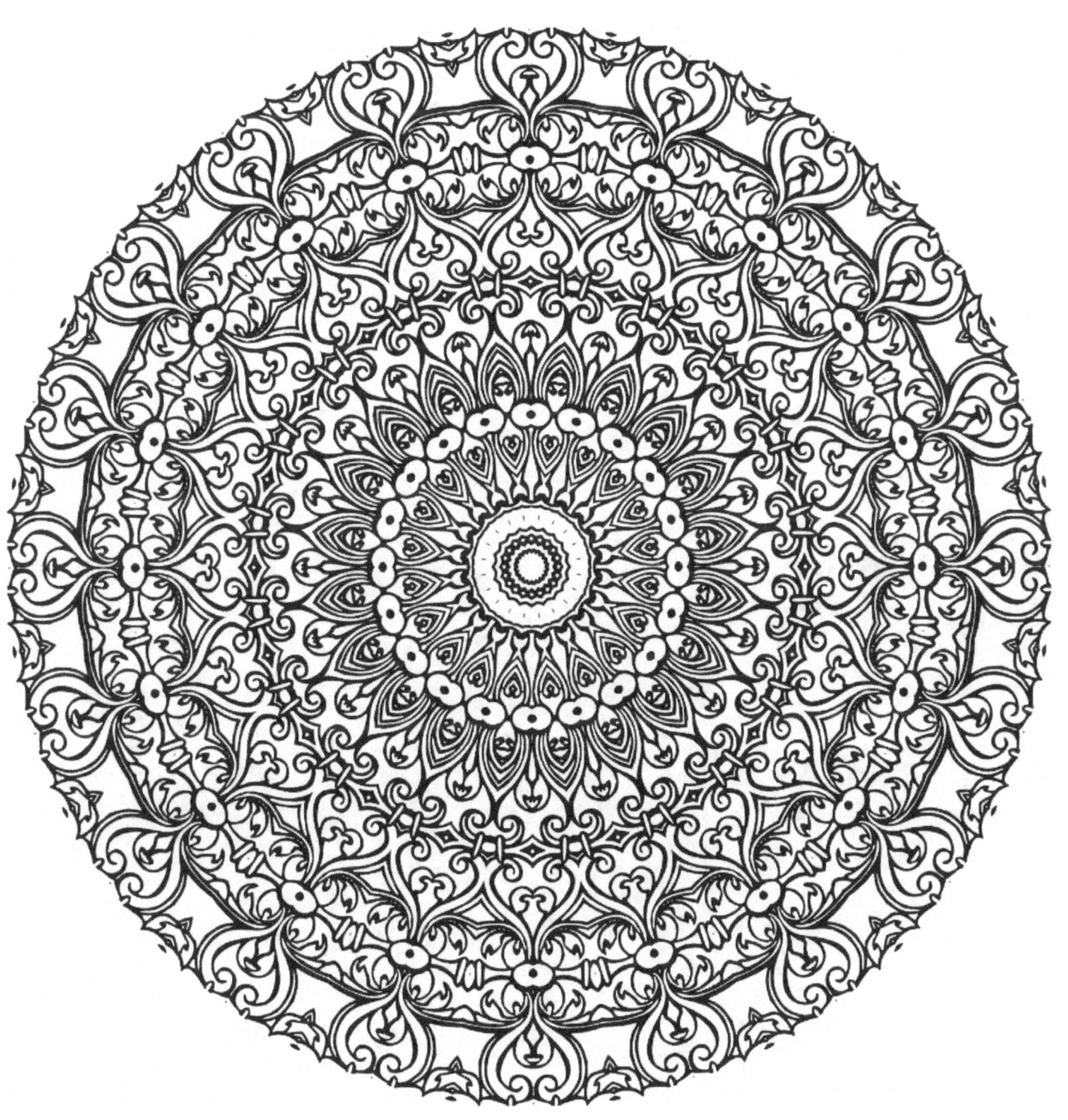

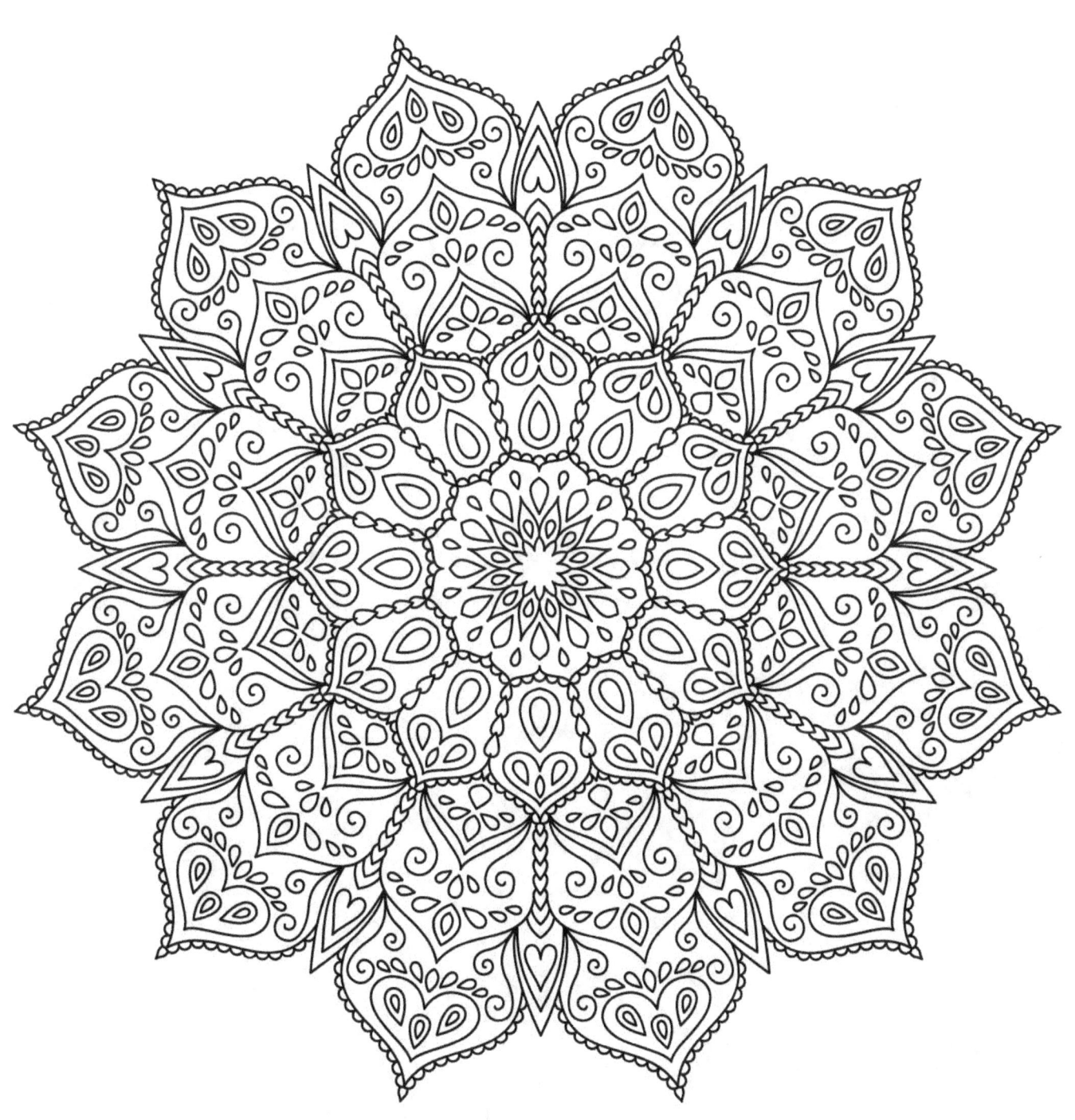

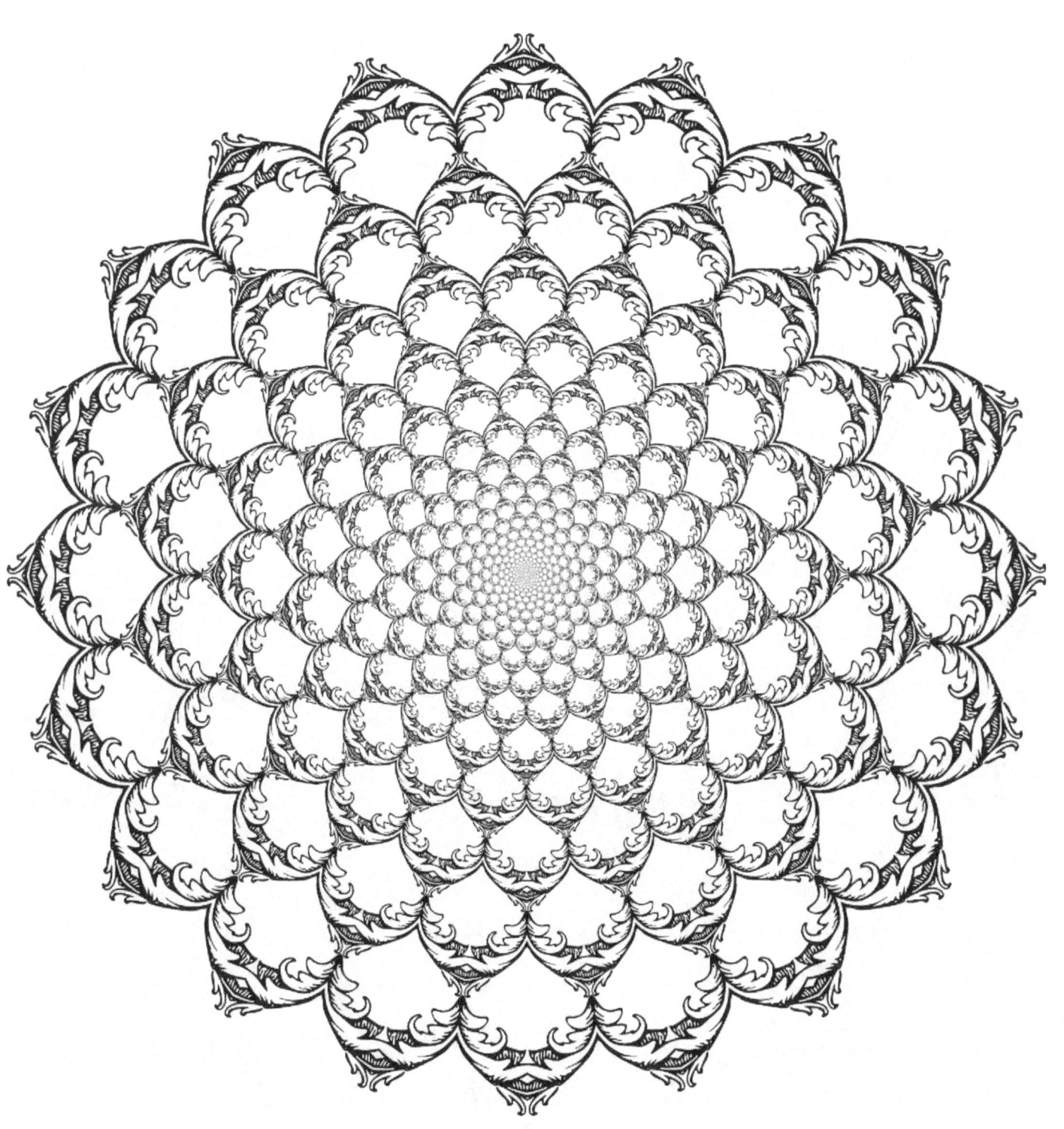

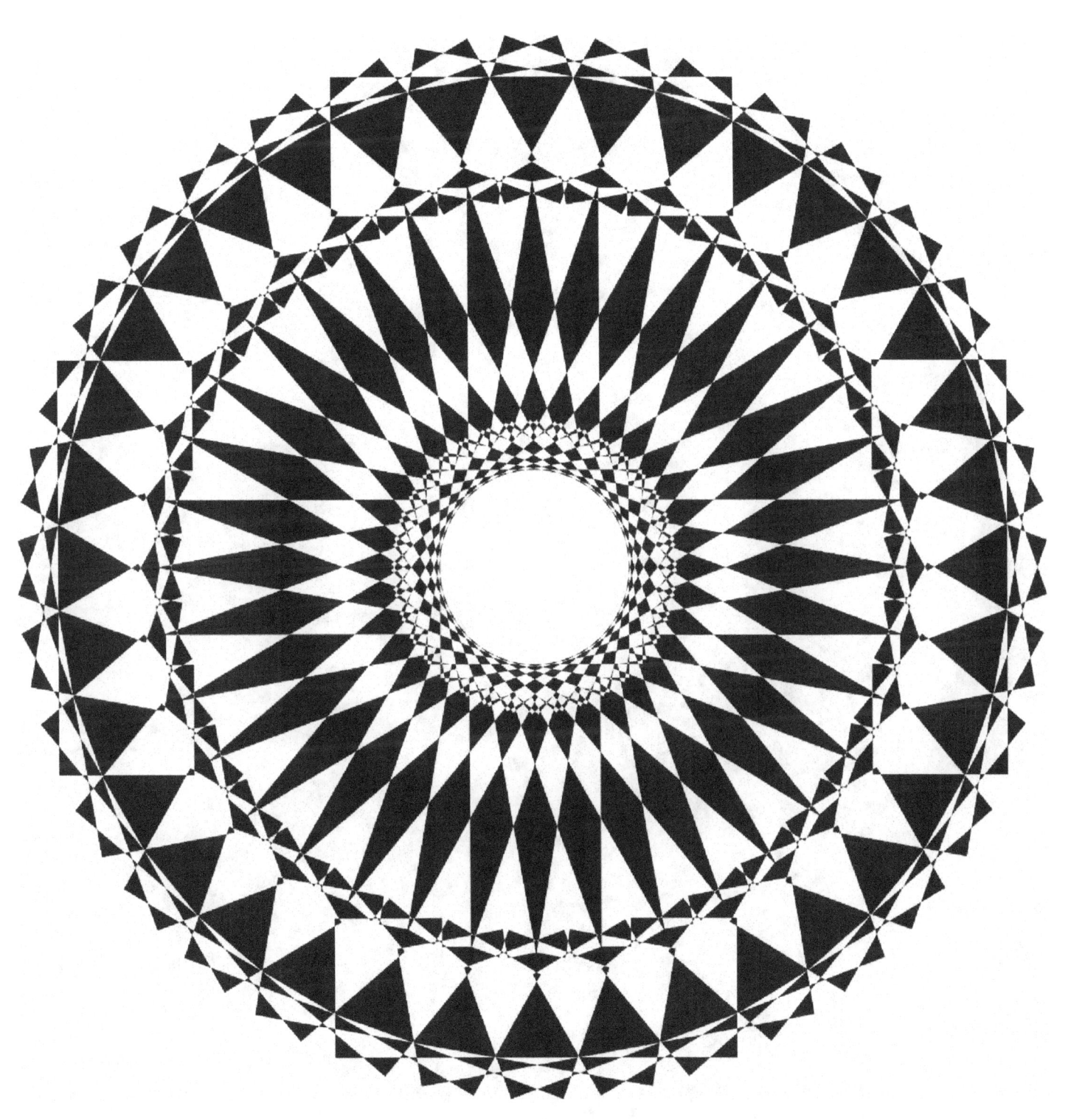

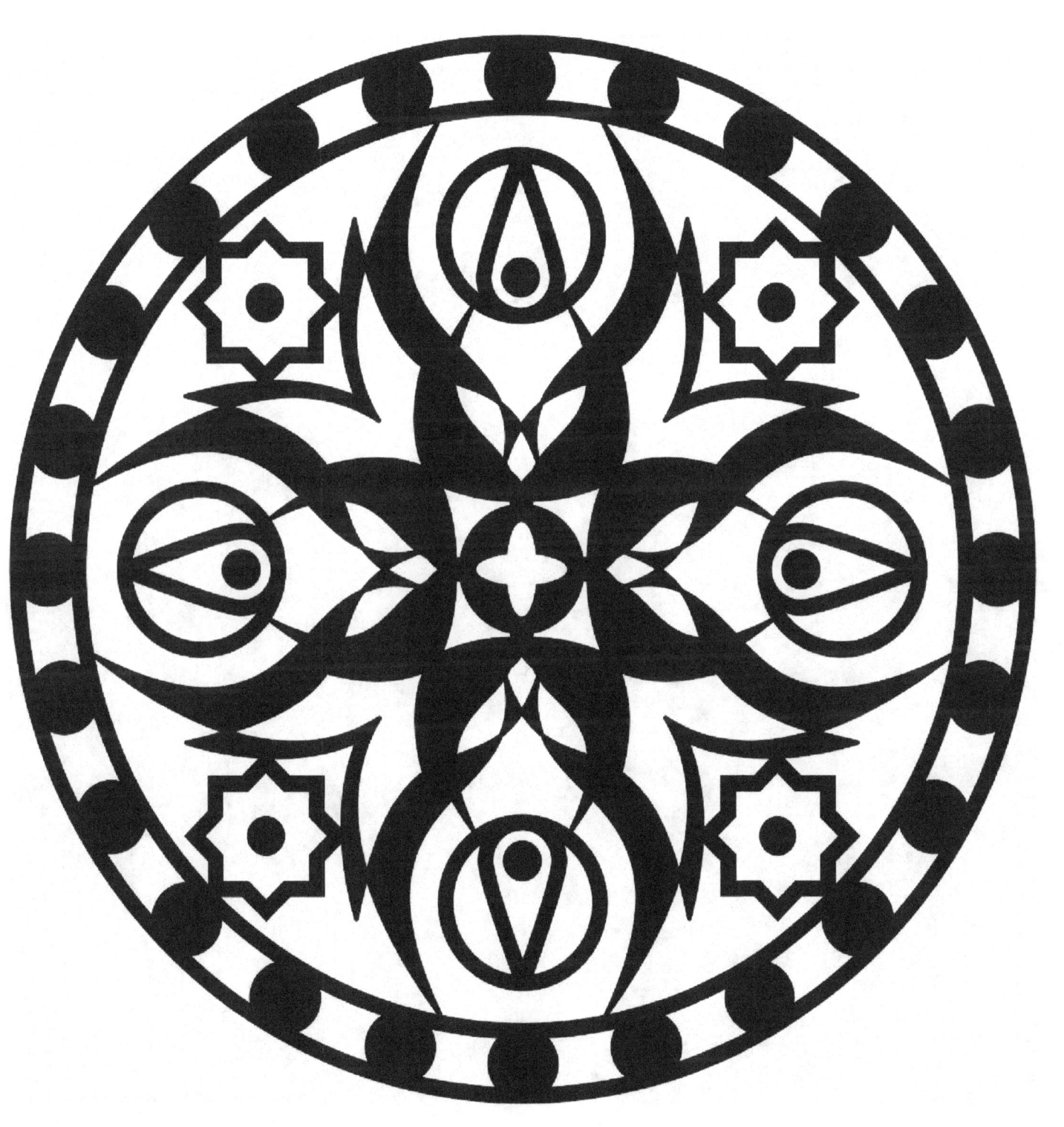

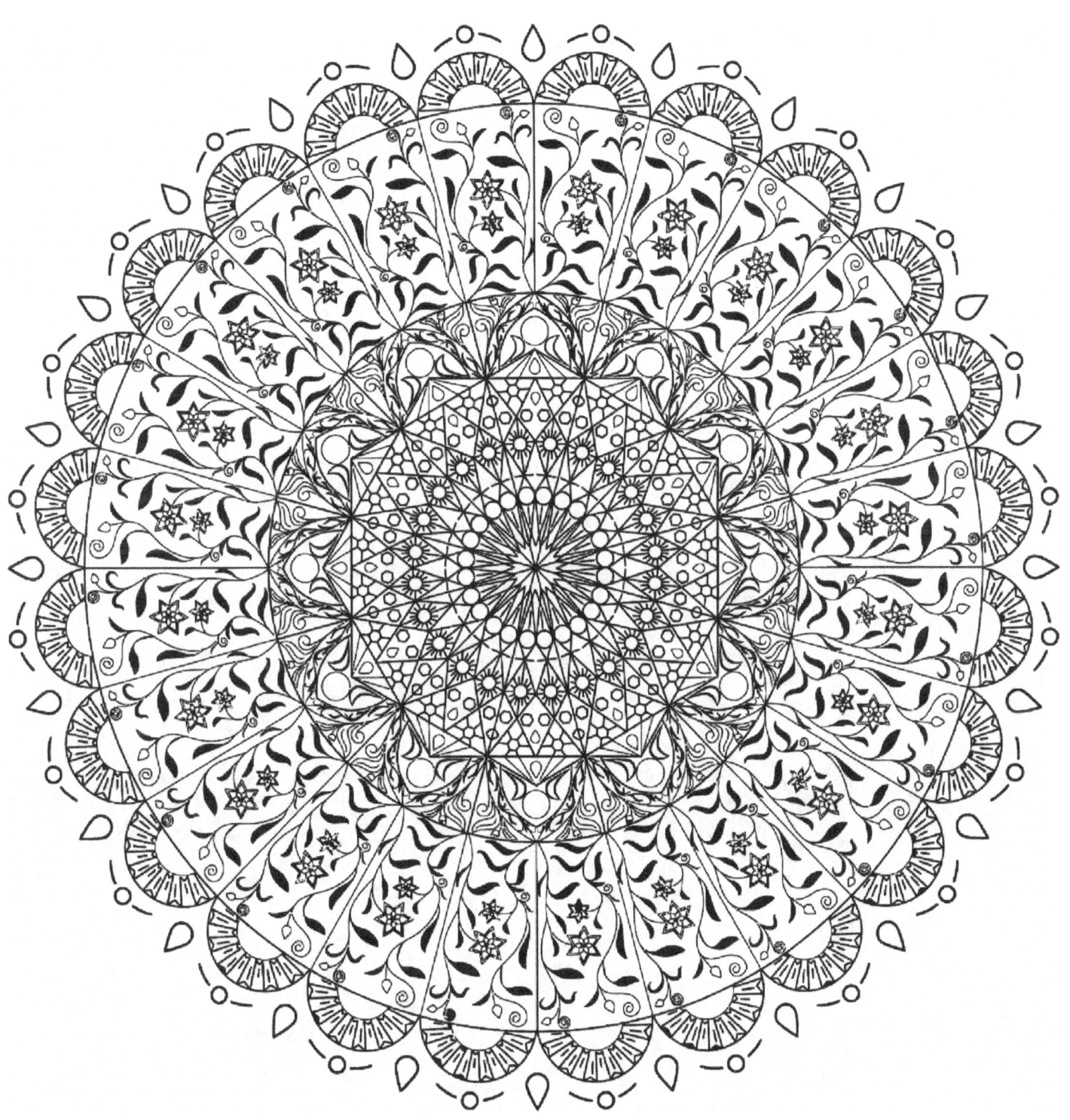

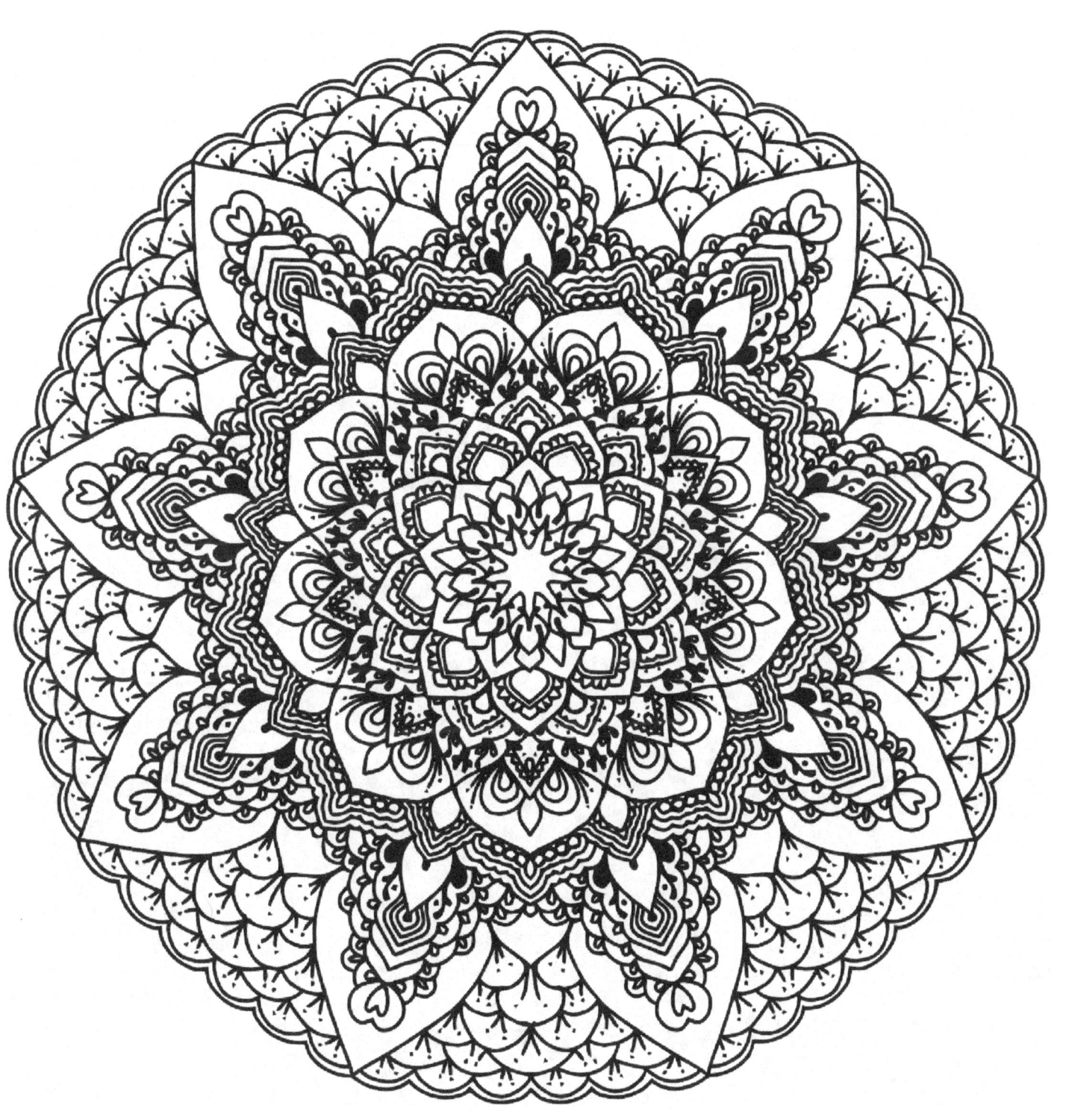

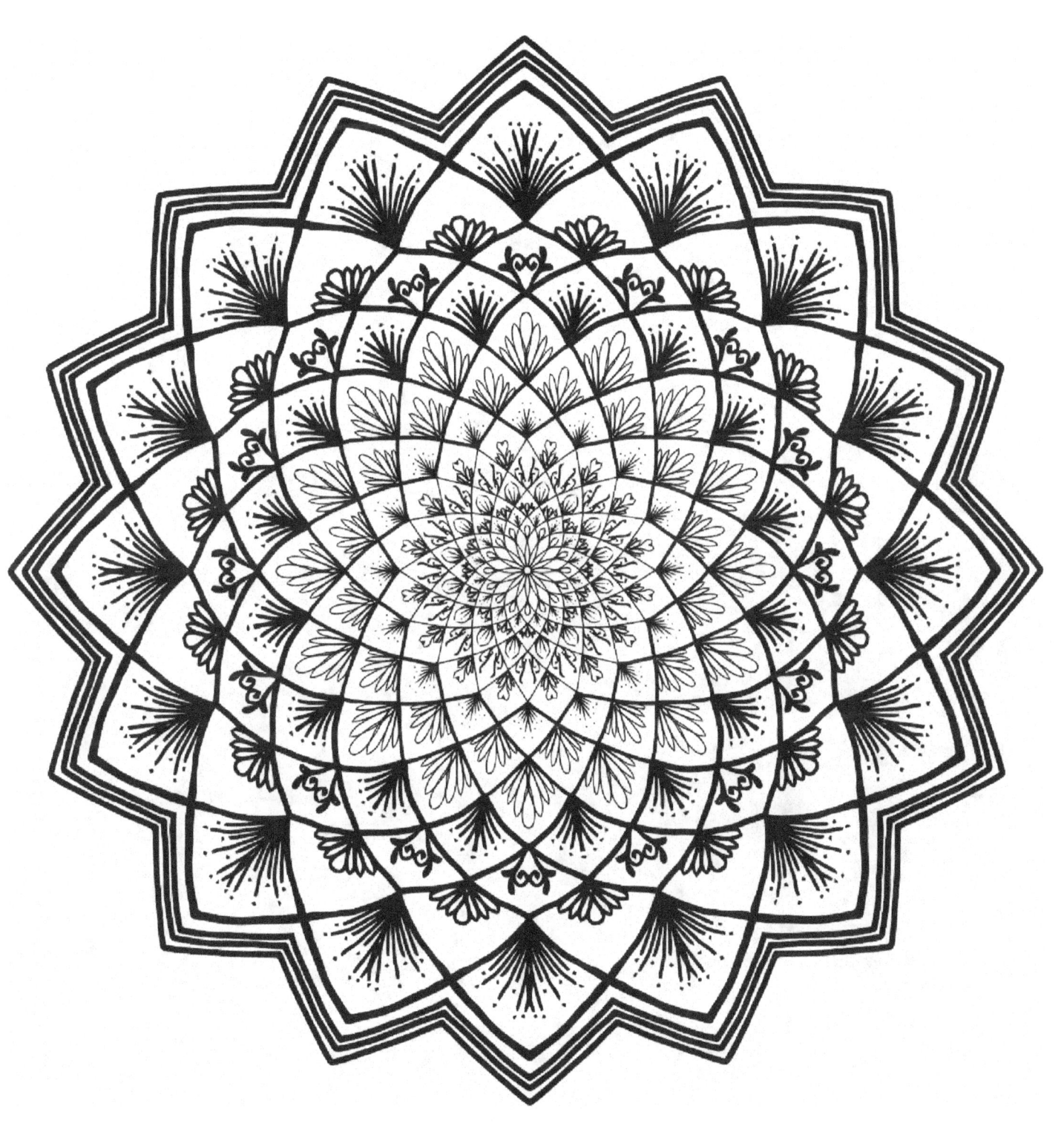

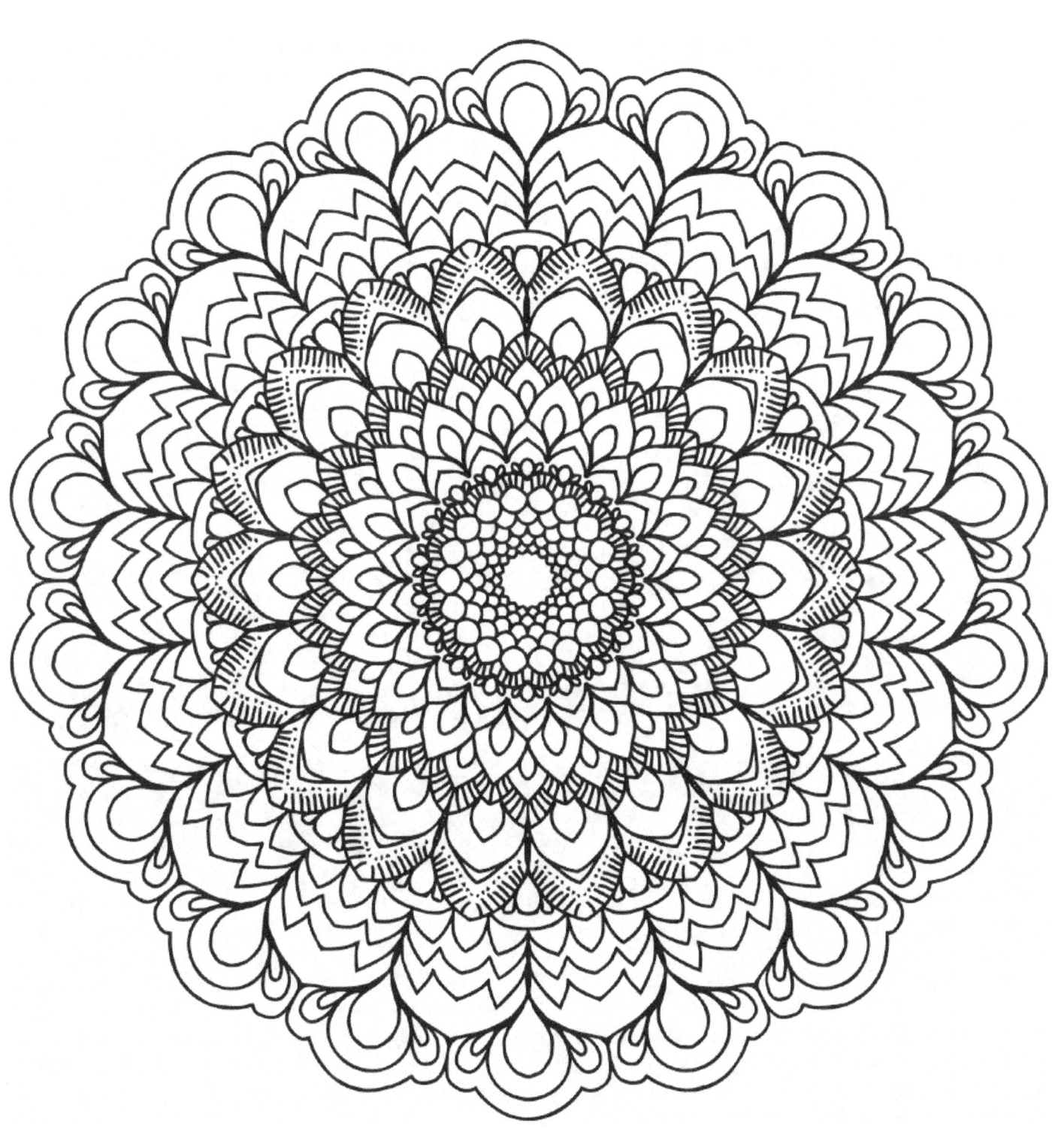

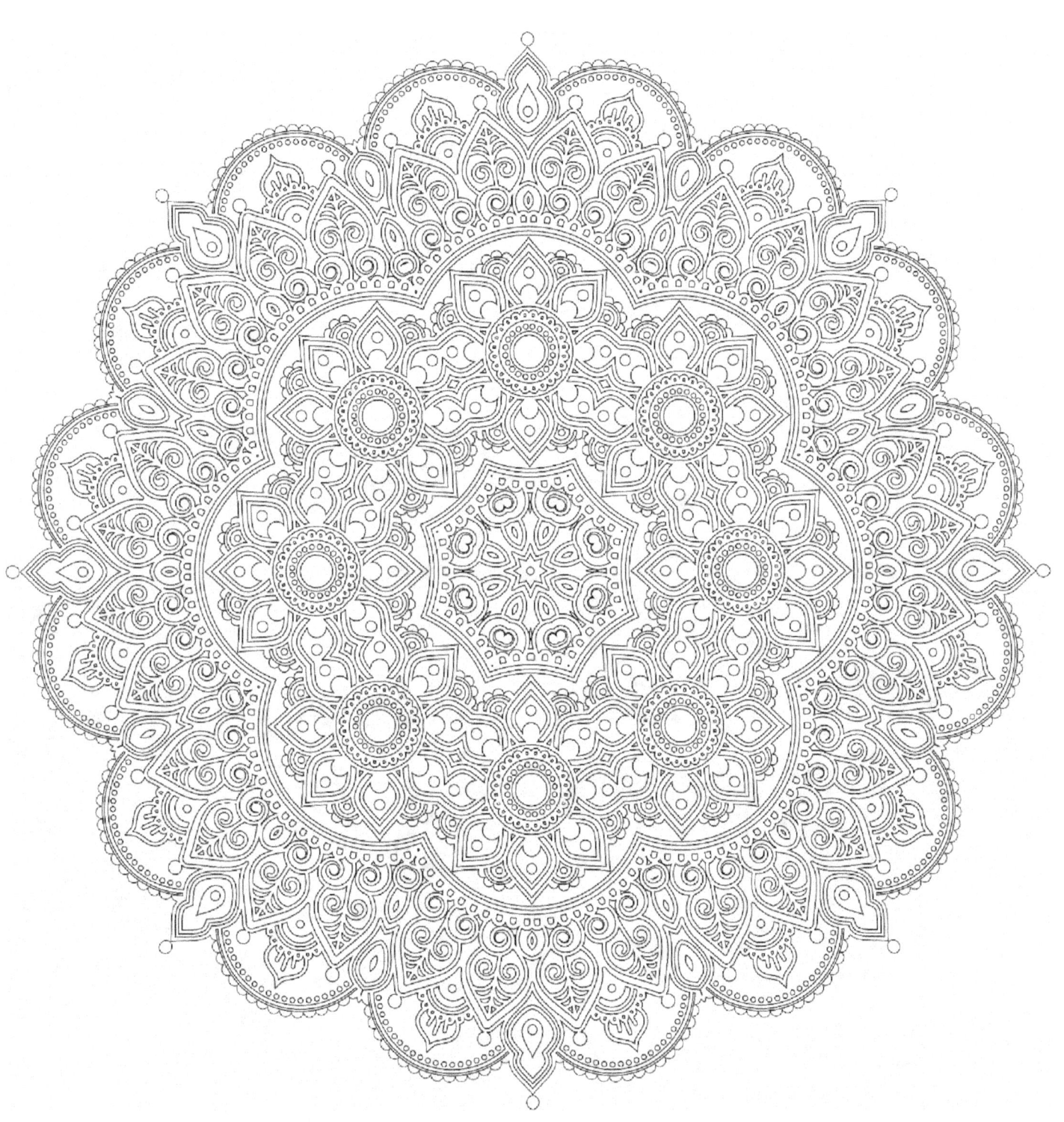

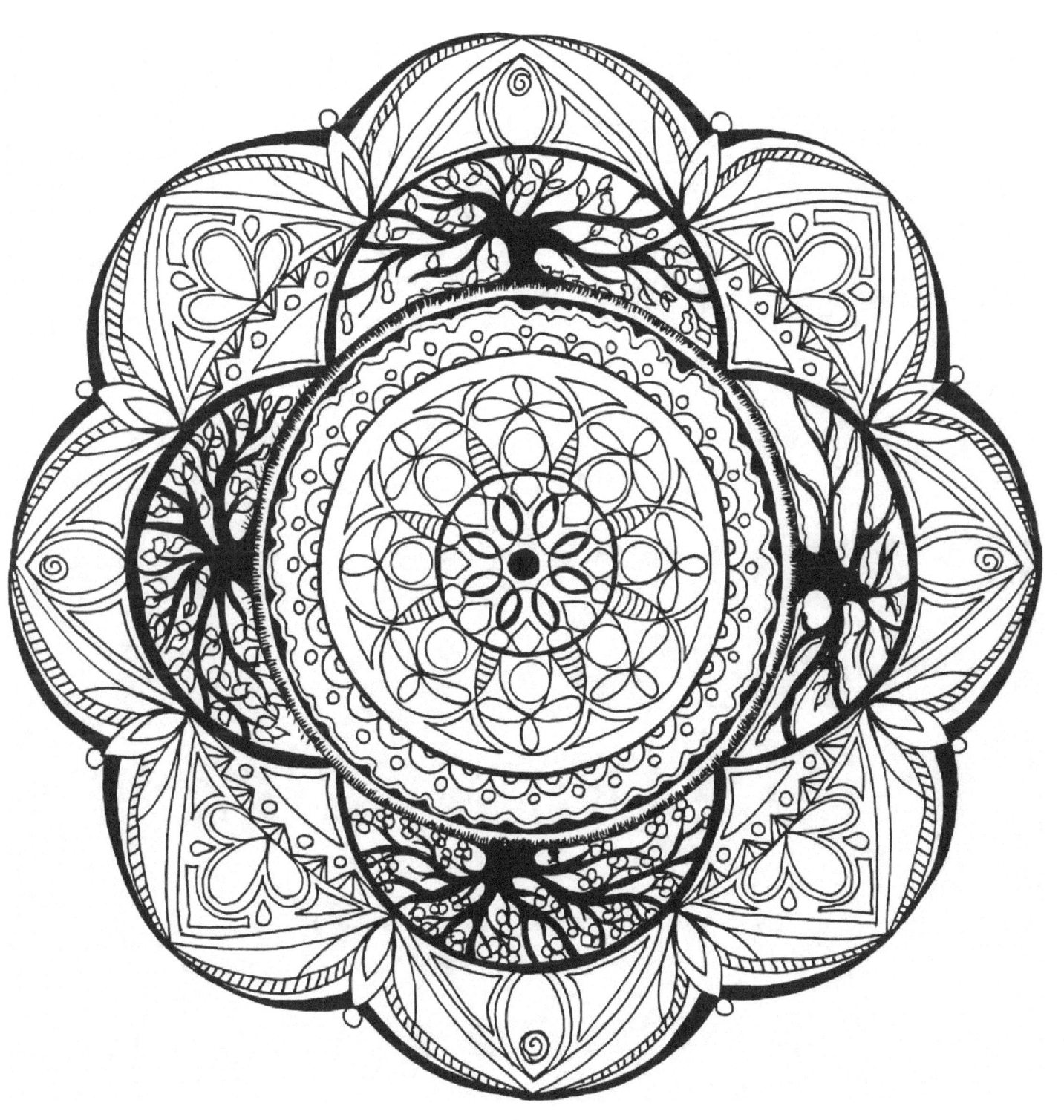

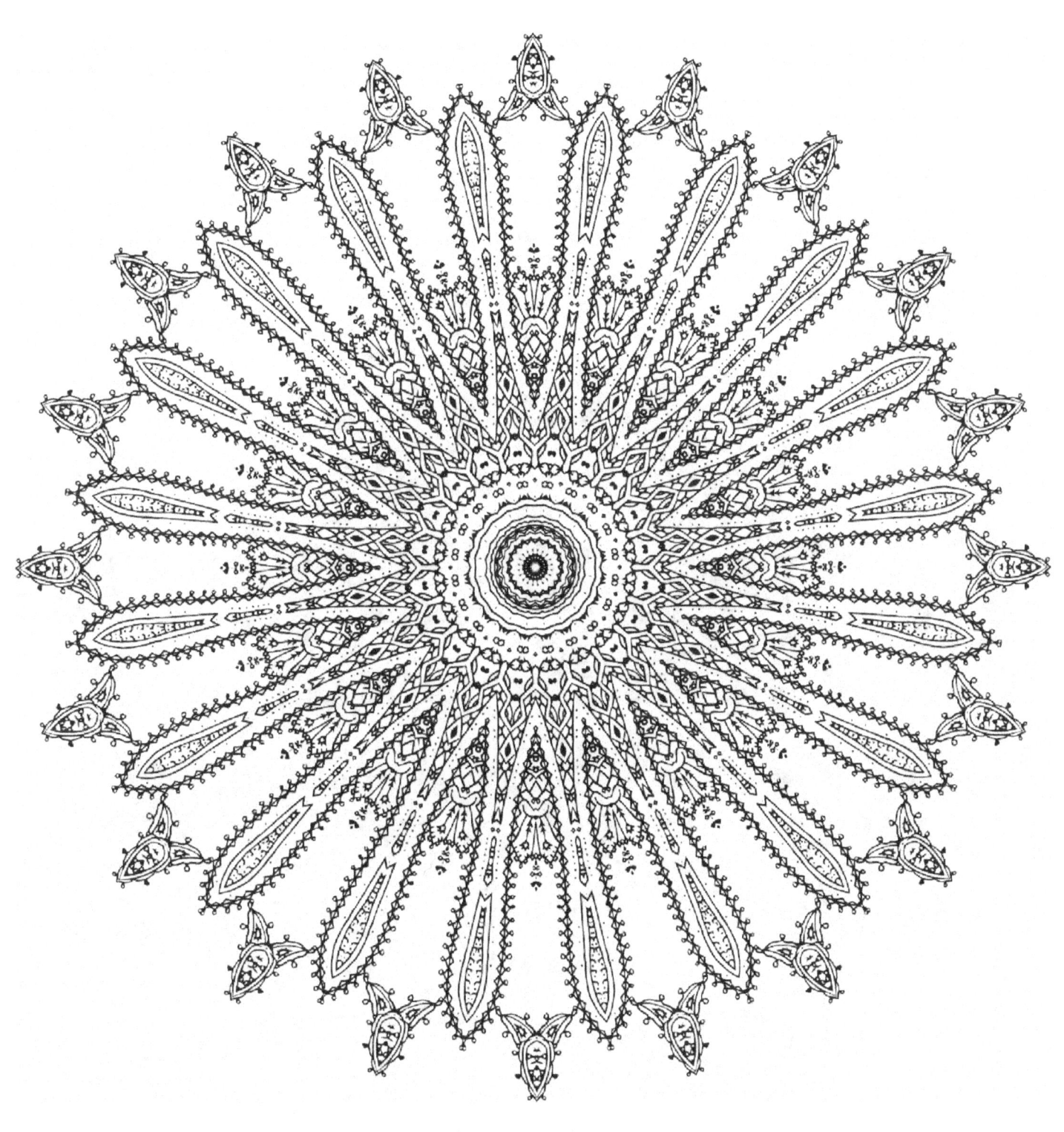

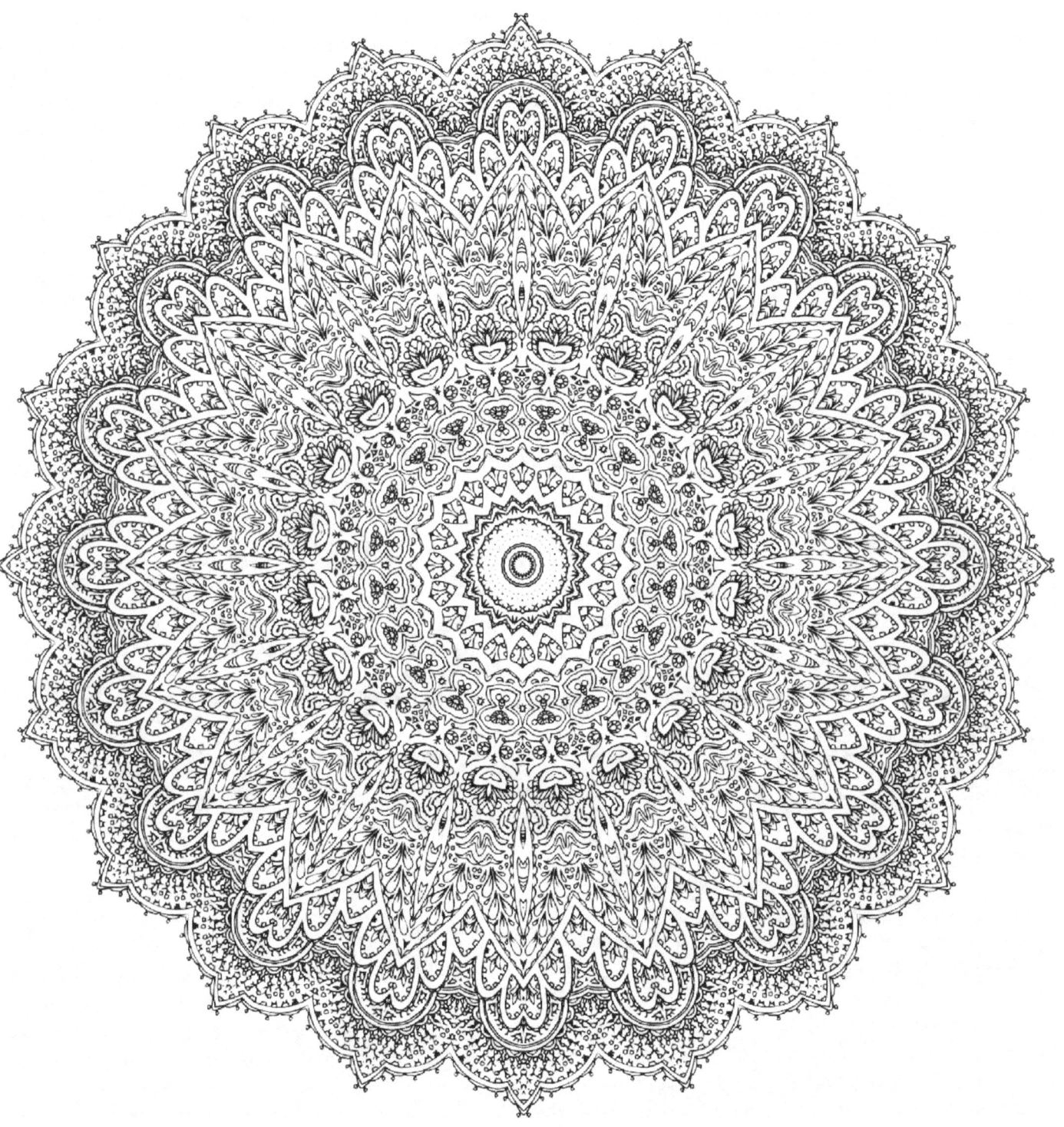

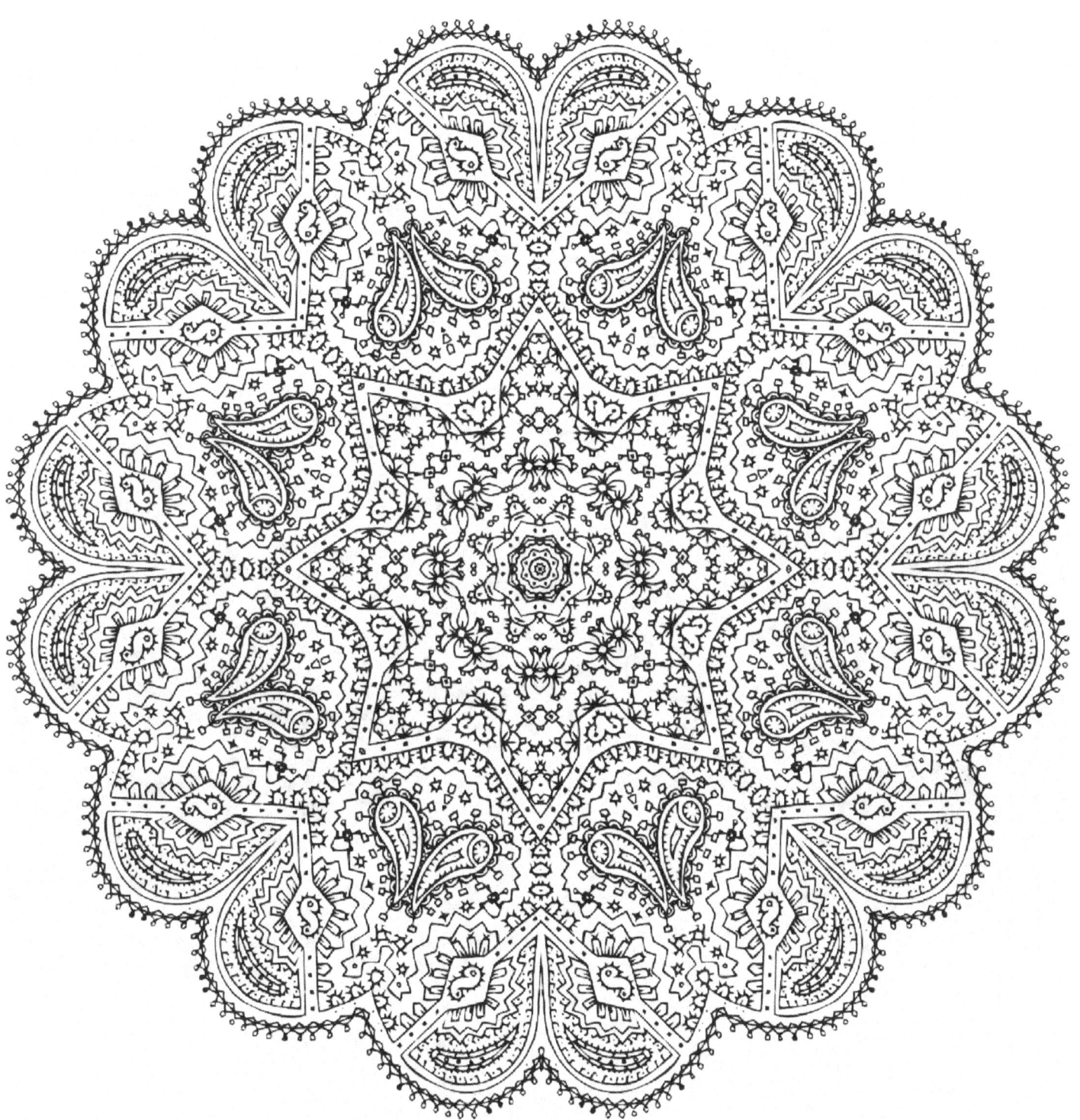

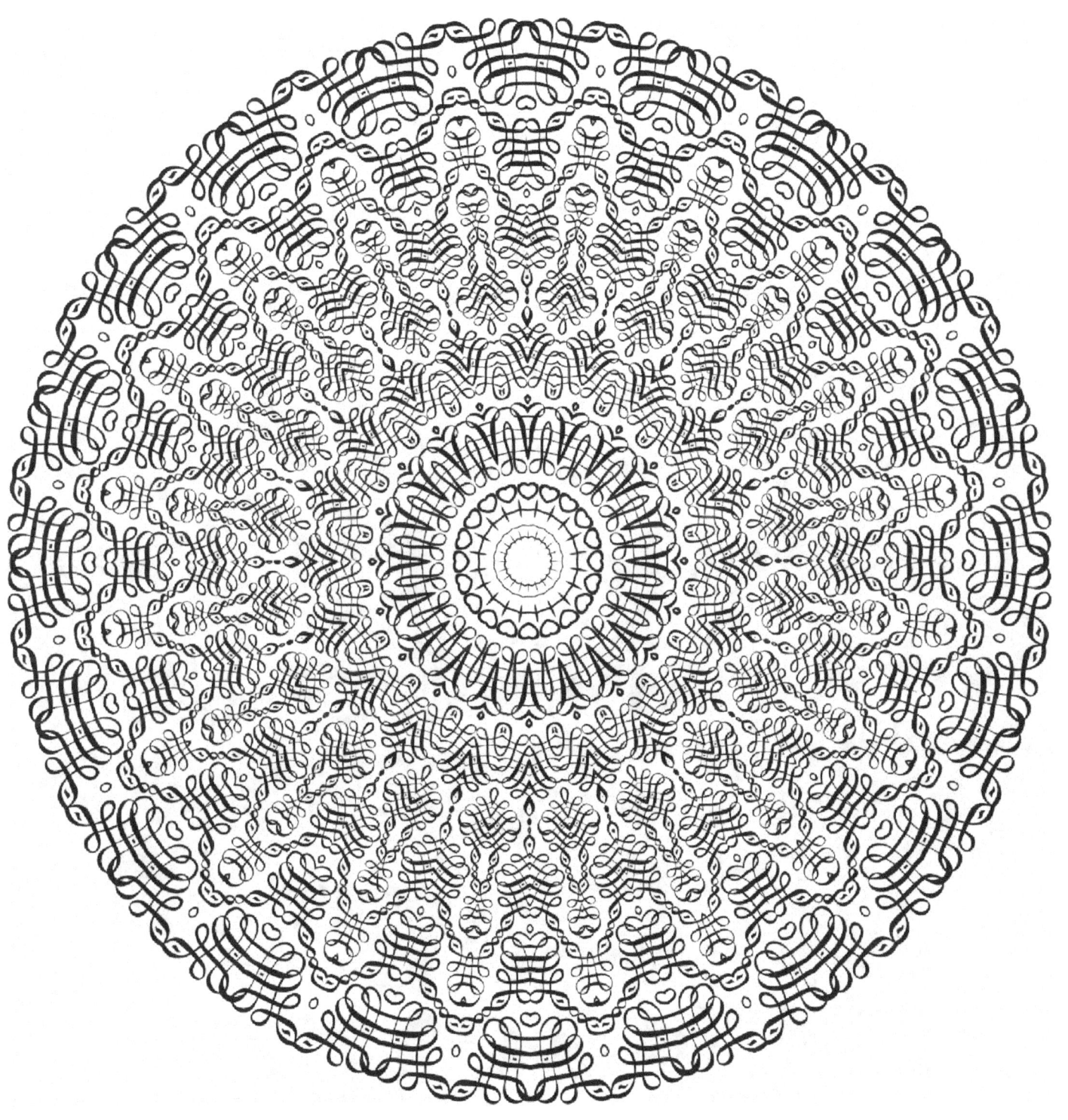

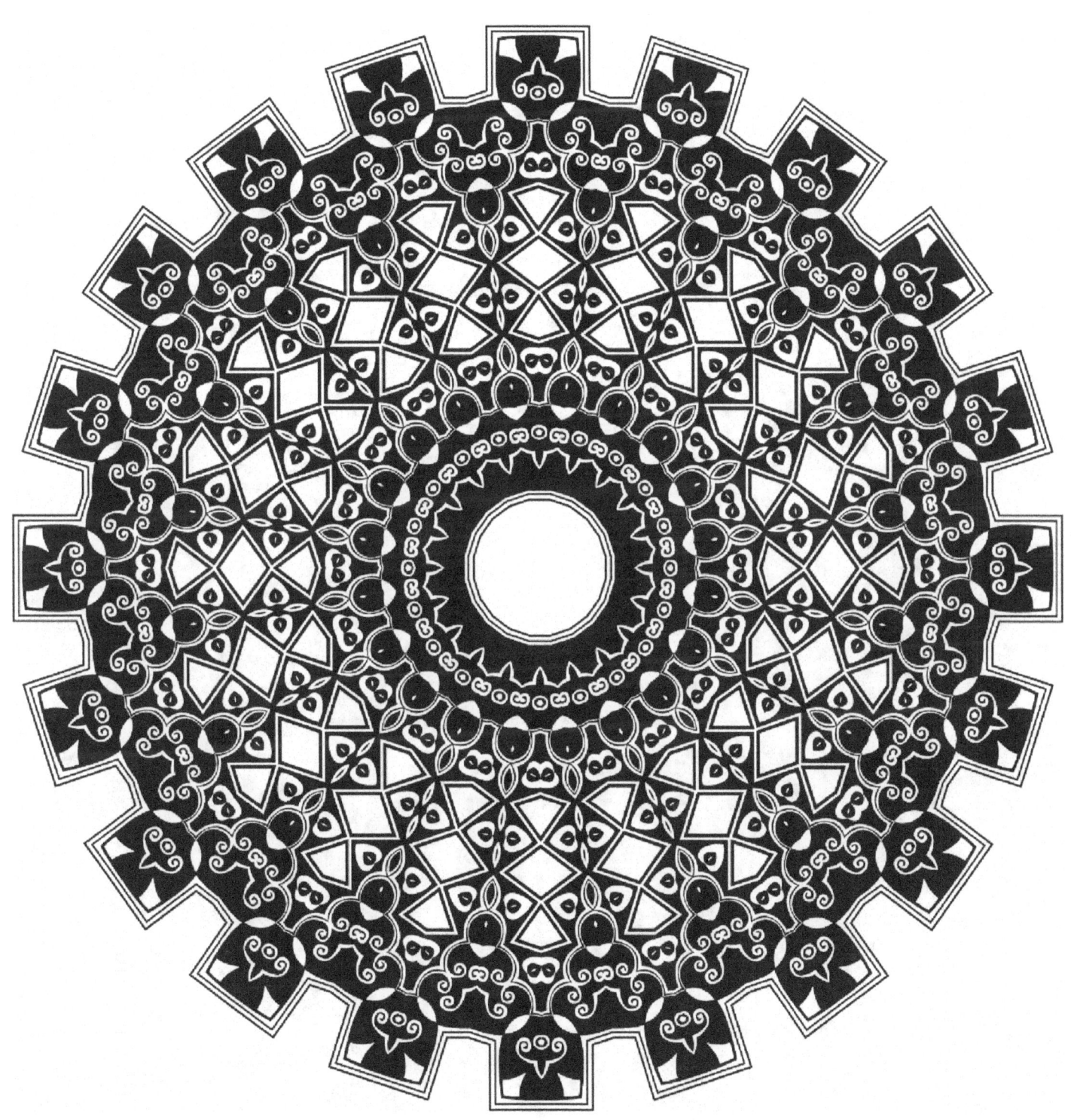

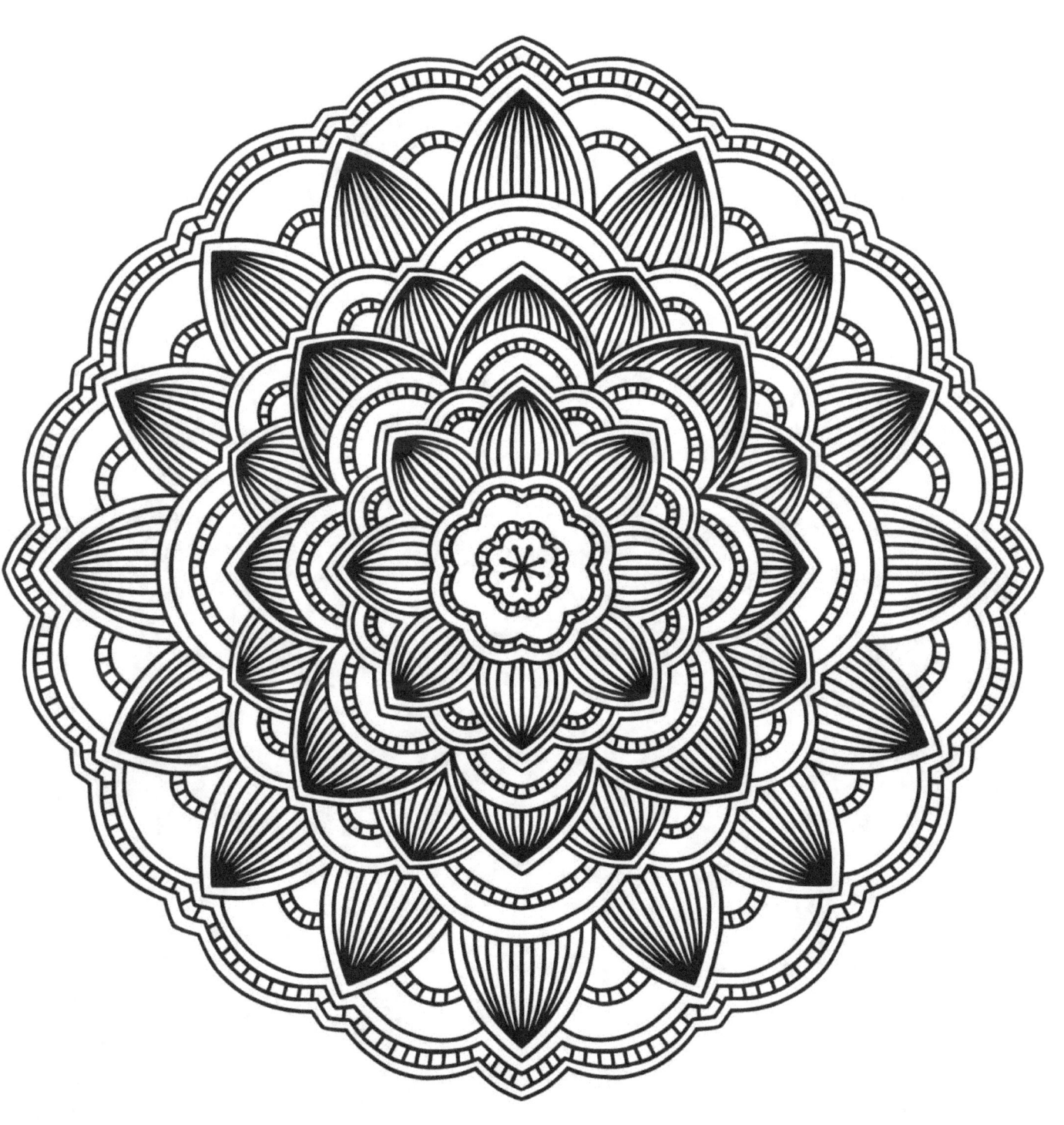

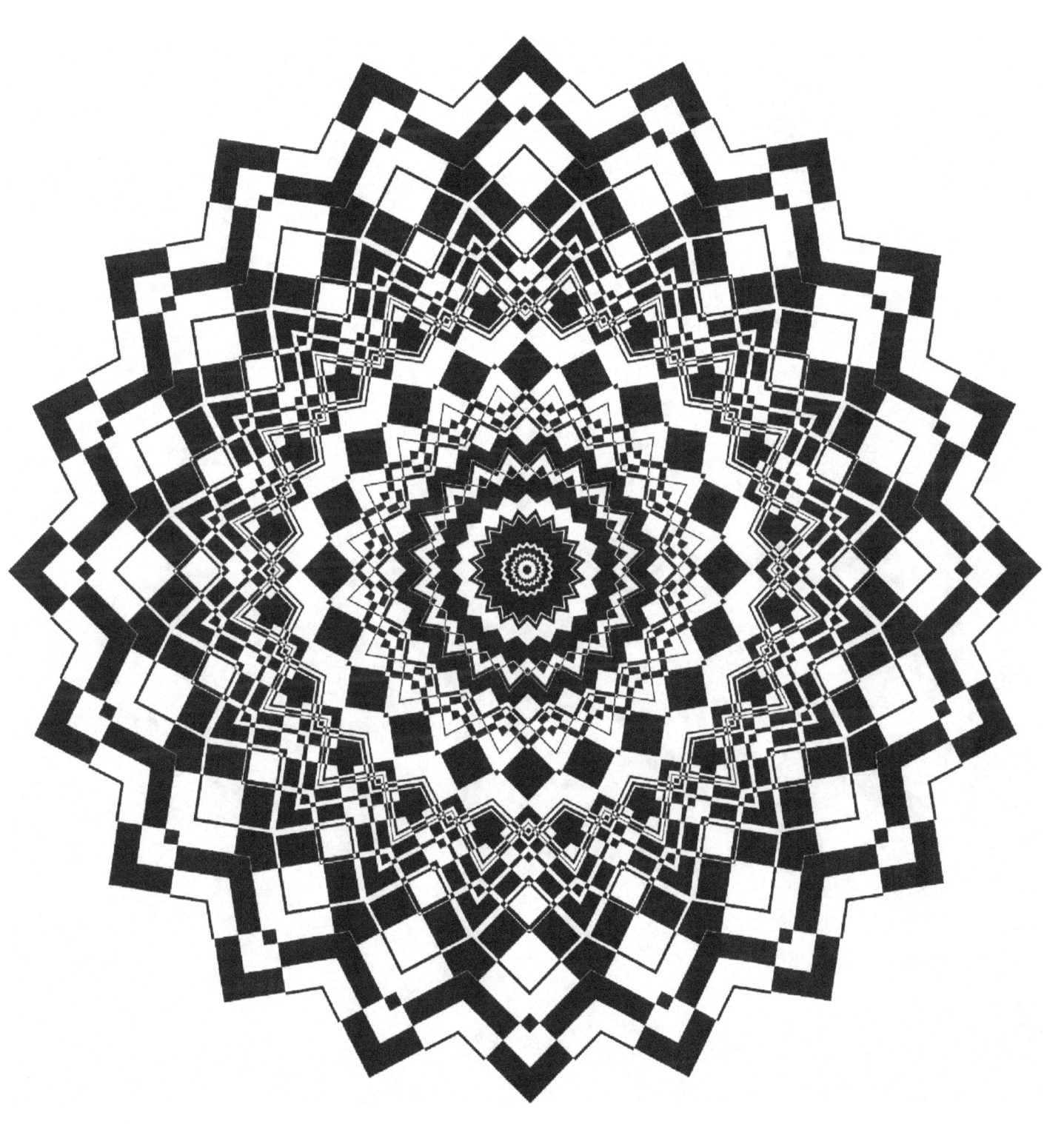

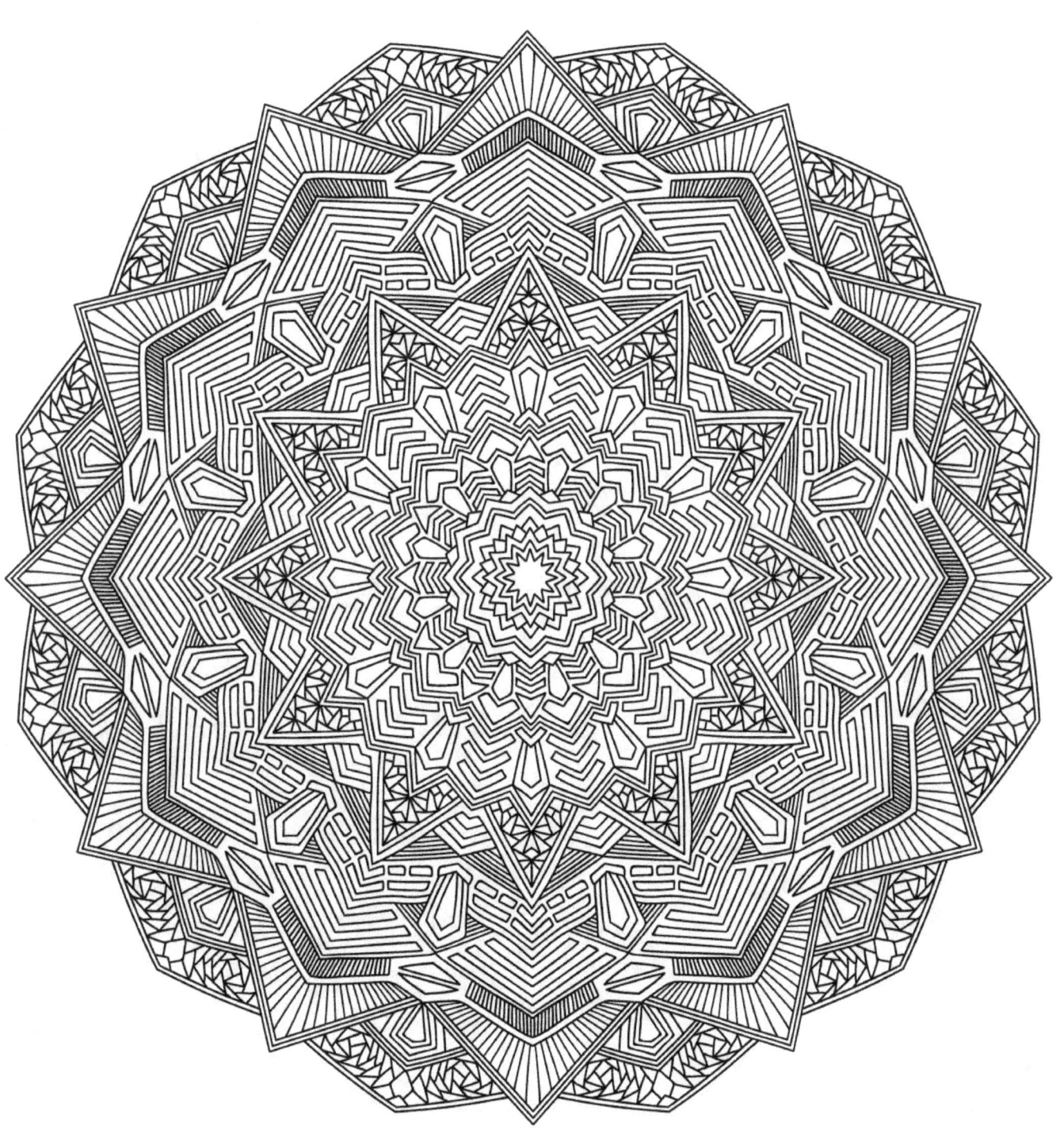

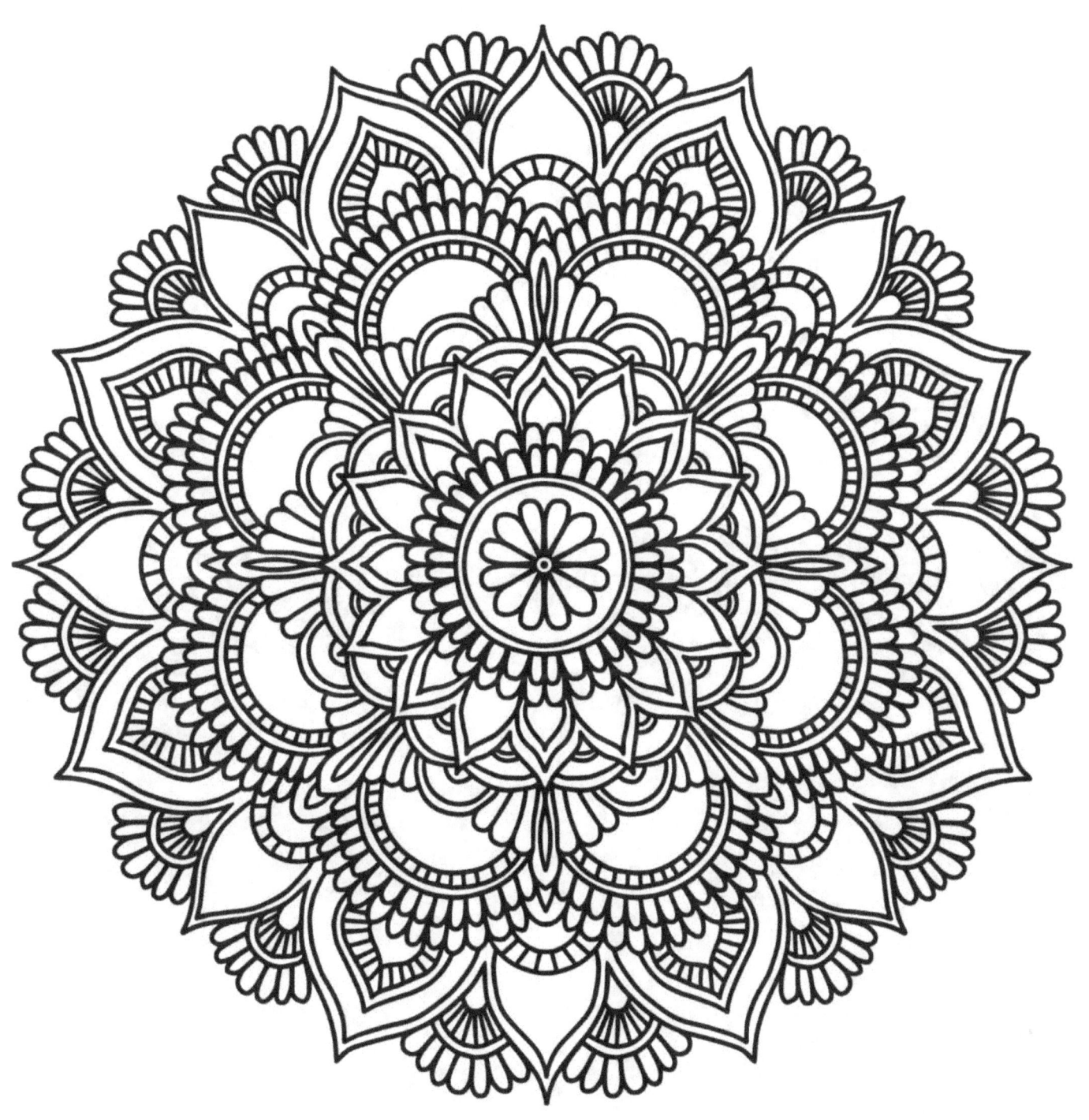

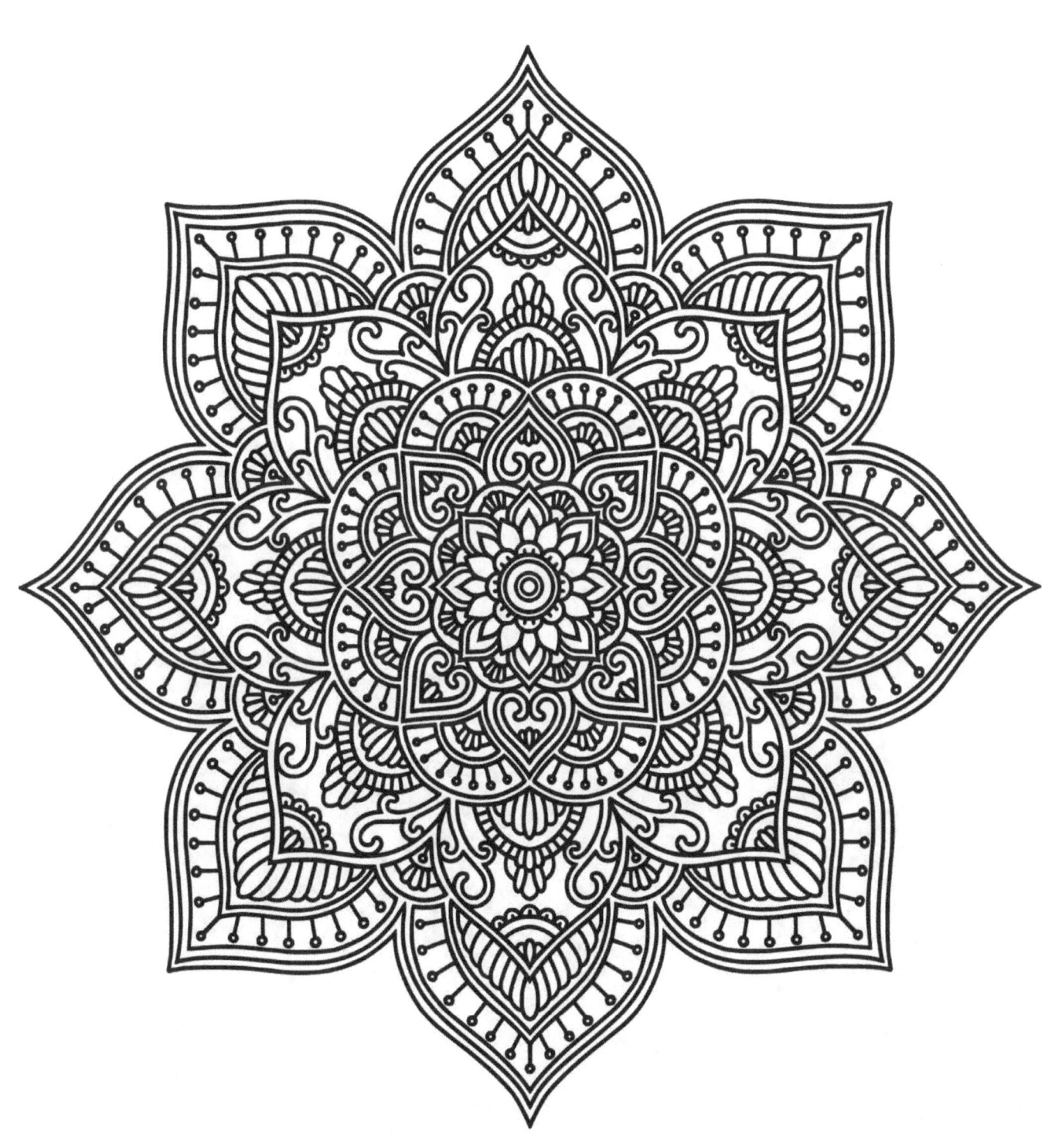

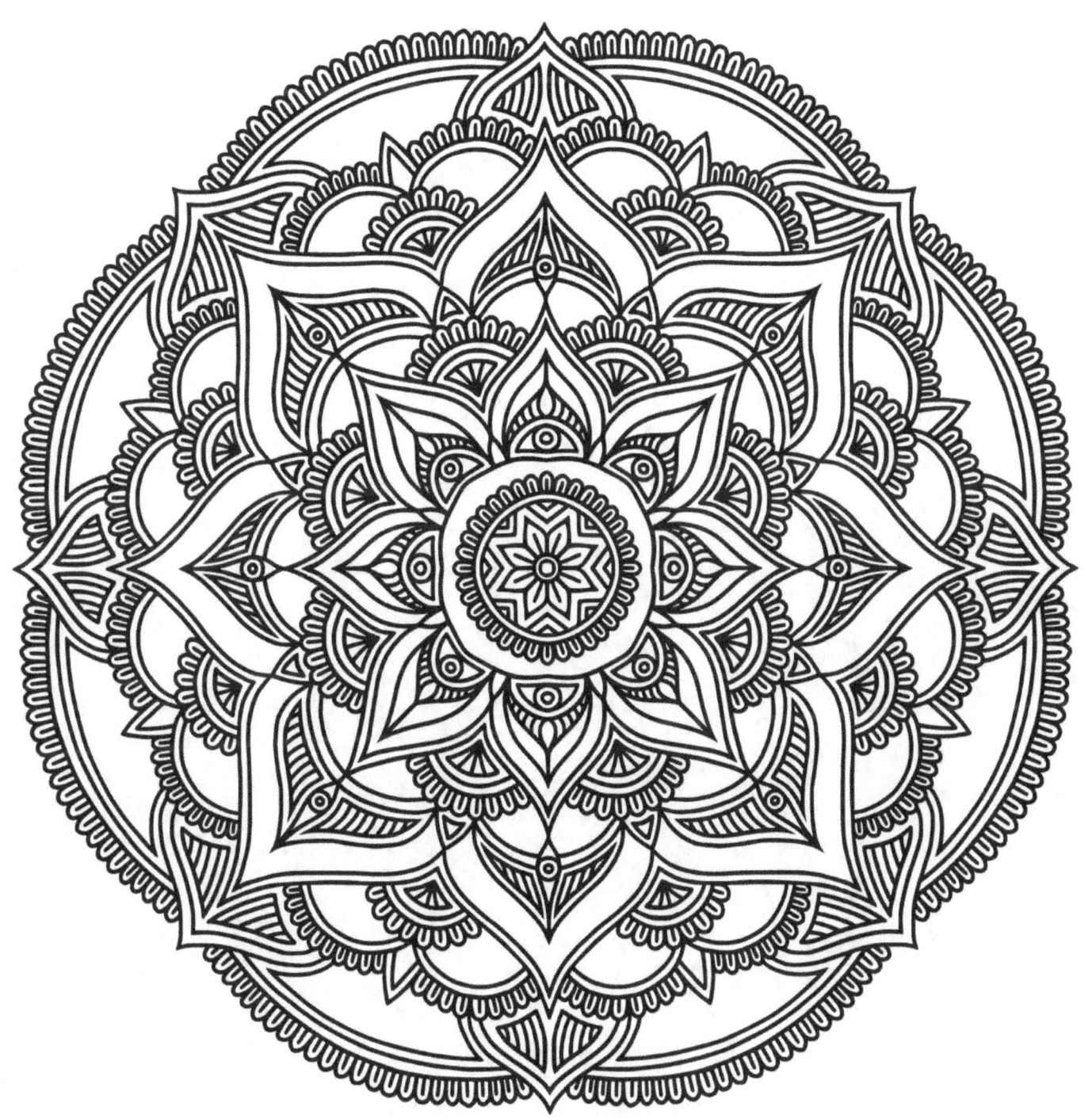

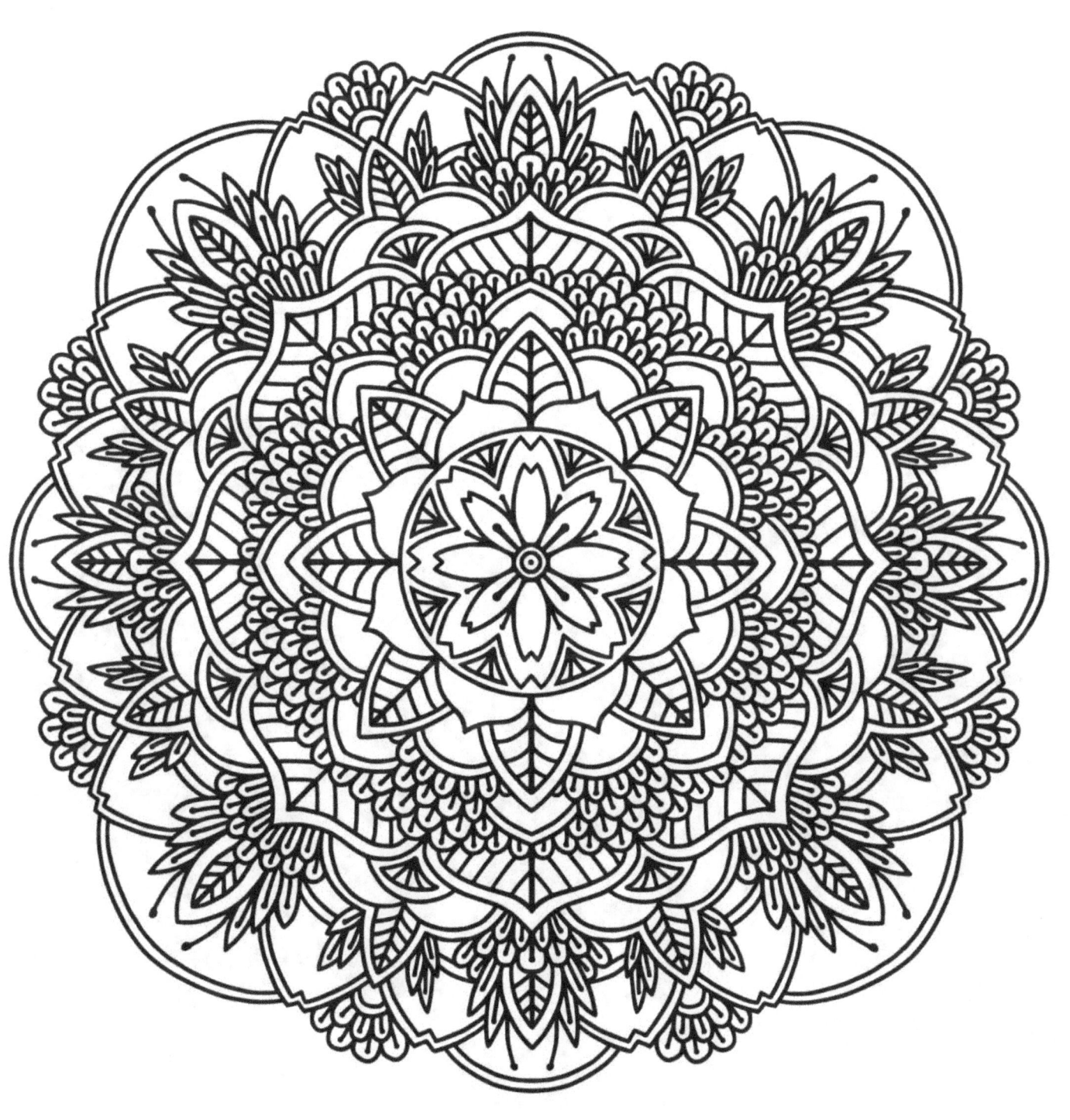

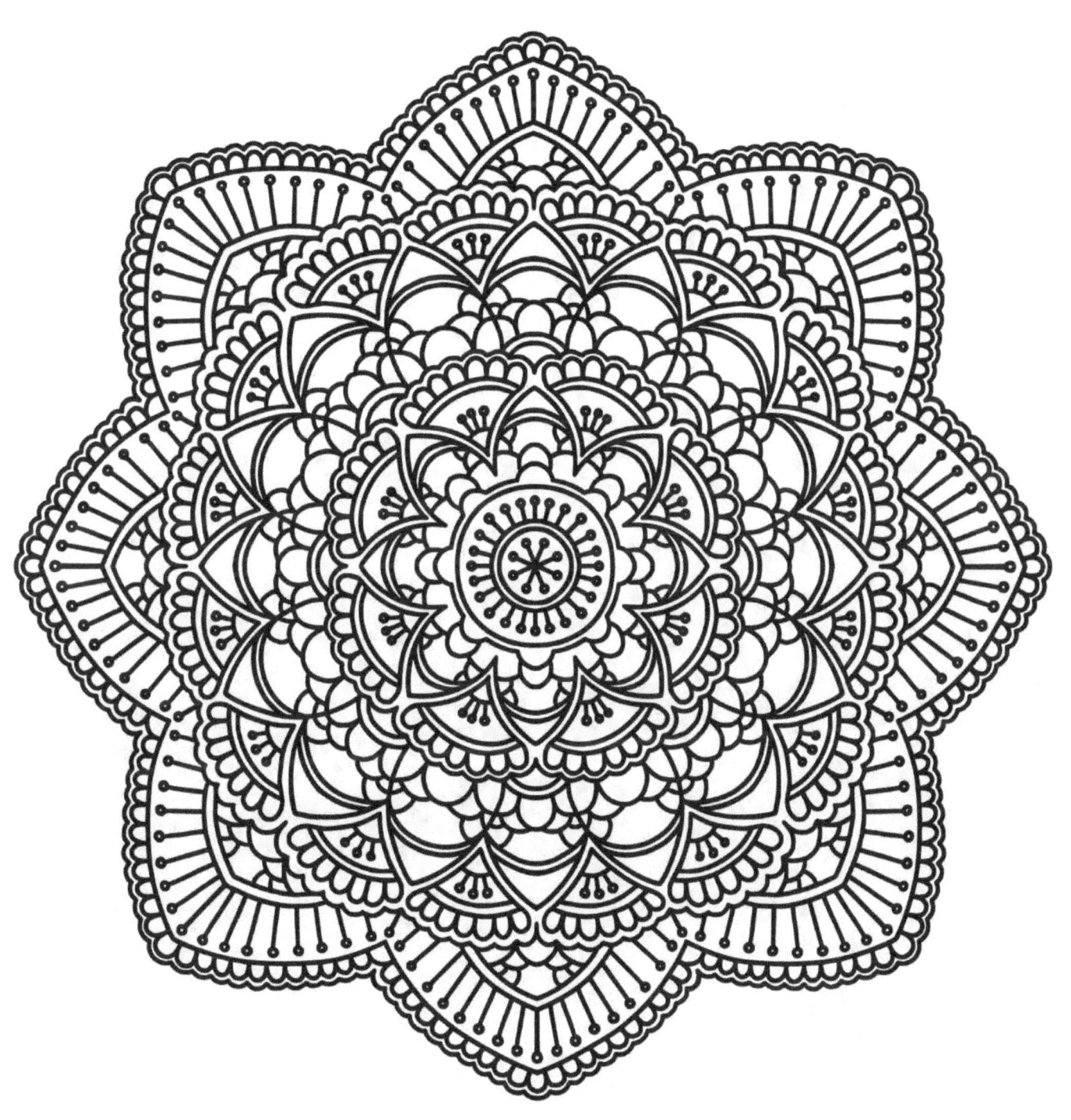

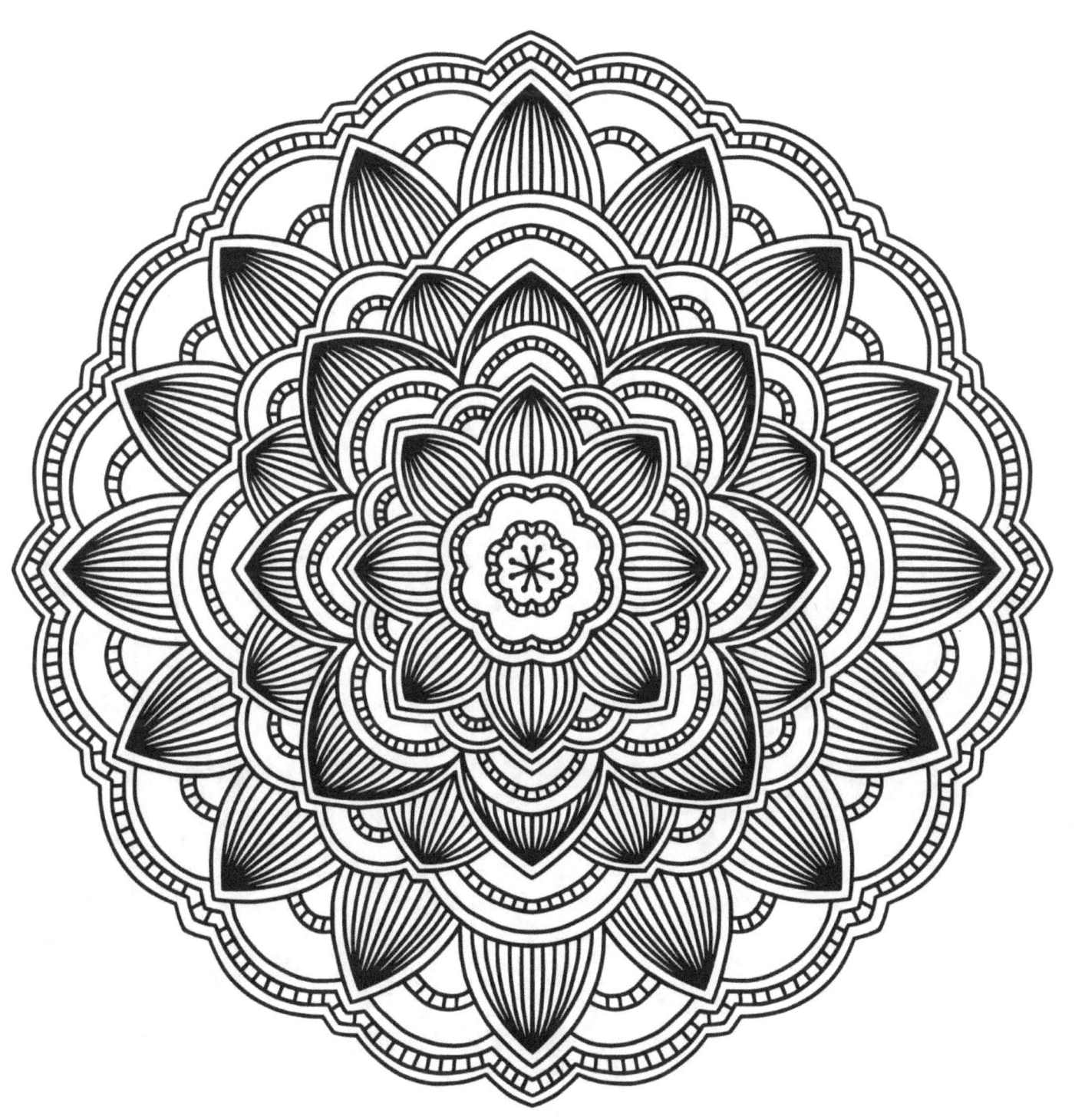

More you may enjoy. Get them now.

Vase Coloring Book
Retro Flower Power
Dancing Girls Coloring Book
Adult Coloring Book - Stress Relief
Flowers, Flowers And More Flowers